# OPENING CRE

Contributors this issue: Simon J. Ballard, Rachel Bellwoar, Dawn Dabell, Jonathon Dabell, David Flack, Brian Gregory, John Harrison, Kev Hurst, Bryan C. Kuriawa, James Lecky, Darren Linder, Stephen Mosley, Kevin Nickelson, Peter Sawford, Joseph Secrett, Ian Taylor, Dr Andrew C. Webber, Steven West. Caricature artwork by Aaron Stielstra.

All articles, photographs and specially produced artwork remain copyright their respective author/photographer/artist. Opinions expressed herein are those of the individual.

Design and Layout: Dawn Dabell
Copy Editor: Jonathon Dabell

Most images in this magazine come from the private collection of Dawn and Jonathon Dabell, or the writer of the corresponding article. Those which do not are made available in an effort to advance understanding of cultural issues pertaining to academic research. We believe this constitutes 'fair use' of any such copyrighted material as provided for in Section 107 of the US Copyright Law. In accordance with Title U.S.C Section 107, this magazine is sold to those who have expressed a prior interest in receiving the included information for research, academic and educational purposes.

Printed globally by Amazon KDP

# A Word from the Editing Room

Welcome, '70s movie lovers!

We're delighted to be back with the eighth issue of our magazine devoted to the films, the filmmakers and the stars of this richest of cinematic decades. Our latest edition is packed with articles covering everything from disaster movies to Woody Allen, from James Bond to Josey Wales, from the jungle hell of *Sorcerer* to the urban hell of *Death Wish*. And there's more - a whole lot more - for your reading pleasure.

The hard part about pulling together the contents for each new issue is not deciding what to put in; it's accepting that some great things are going to have to be left out. That's one of the great things about '70s cinema, the sheer breadth and depth of interesting titles. It truly is a veritable treasure trove of goodies.

For readers who don't yet know, we run a sister magazine called 'Cinema of the '80s'. Issue #2 was recently published and has been selling well. A third issue will be on the way imminently. If '80s cinema floats your boat, we'd be delighted to welcome you to our ever-growing readership.

2022 drew to a close recently, and it was sad to look back and reflect on the big names we'd lost over the course of the year. At times, it feels like our favourite stars are slipping off the mortal coil at an alarming rate. It's easy to convince yourself there are none left. It was a pleasant surprise, therefore, when we realised whilst writing this editorial that every one of the actors pictured around the perimeter of this page is (at the time of writing, at least) still with us. May they remain alive and well for a good few years yet!

Until Issue 9, farewell. Happy reading!

Dawn and Jonathon Dabell

# Remembering Raquel Welch (1940-2023)

On February 15th, 2023, Raquel Welch died at her home in Los Angeles after a short illness. She was 82.

Welch had risen to fame as a screen star and international sex symbol in the '60s, thanks largely to iconic roles (and outfits) in *Fantastic Voyage* and *One Million Years B.C.* (both 1966). She spent the rest of that decade and most of the '70s enjoying big roles in a run of major films. She is credited with transforming America's notion of 'the feminine ideal' into its current state, marking a shift from the 'blonde bombshell' image perfected and popularised by the likes of Marilyn Monroe and Jayne Mansfield in the '50s.

Her '70s film credits were:
Myra Breckinridge (1970)
Hannie Caulder (1971)
Sin (1971)
Fuzz (1972)
Kansas City Bomber (1972)
Bluebeard (197?)
The Last of Sheila (1973)
The Three Musketeers (1973)
The Four Musketeers (1974)
The Wild Party (1975)
Mother, Jugs & Speed (1976)
The Prince and the Pauper (1977)
L'Animal (1977)

So long Miss Welch, and thanks for the memories.

# In Memoriam

**Ruggero Deodato (1939-2022)**
Director, known for *Live Like a Cop, Die Like a Man* (1976) and *Jungle Holocaust* (1977).

**Melinda Dillon (1939-2022)**
Actress, known for *Slap Shot* (1977) and *Close Encounters of the Third Kind* (1977).

**Jean-Luc Godard (1930-2022)**
Director, known for *Tout va bien* (1972) and *Here and Elsewhere* (1976).

**Mike Hodges (1932-2022)**
Director, known for *Get Carter* (1971) and *The Terminal Man* (1974).

**Angela Lansbury (1925-2022)**
Actress, known for *Bedknobs and Broomsticks* (1971) and *Death on the Nile* (1978).

**Gina Lollobrigida (1927-2023)**
Actress, known for *Bad Man's River* (1971) and *King, Queen, Knave* (1972).

**Stuart Margolin (1940-2022)**
Actor, known for *Kelly's Heroes* (1970) and *Death Wish* (1974).

**Leslie Phillips (1924-2022)**
Actor, known for *The Magnificent Seven Deadly Sins* (1971) and *Spanish Fly* (1976).

**Sylvia Sims (1934-2023)**
Actress, known for *Asylum* (1972) and *The Tamarind Seed* (1974).

**Cindy Williams (1947-2023)**
Actress, known for *American Graffiti* (1973) and *The Conversation* (1974).

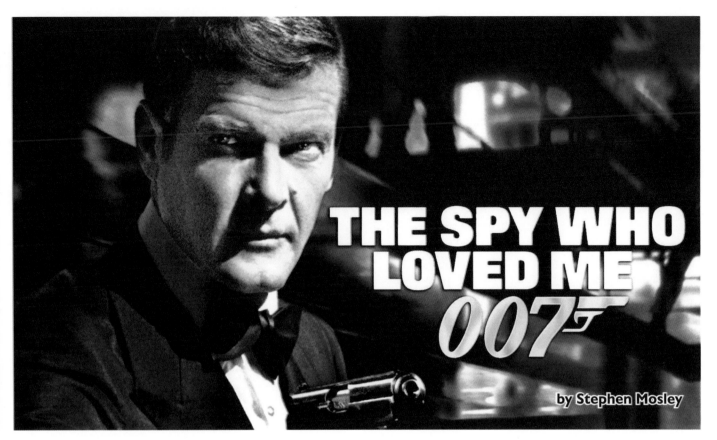

# THE SPY WHO LOVED ME 007

by Stephen Mosley

*The Spy Who Loved Me* was the tenth entry in Eon Productions' James Bond series, and the third to star Roger Moore as the debonair 007. Indeed, the film was Moore's personal favourite of his Bond adventures and is, in this author's opinion, the greatest of them all. Yet the road to its production was not as smooth as Moore's performance. For one thing, the novel from which it took its name was despised, not only by critics but also by the author himself.

First published in 1962, 'The Spy Who Loved Me' was the tenth of Ian Fleming's fourteen James Bond books. When producers Albert R. Broccoli and Harry Saltzman began filming the literary series that same year, Fleming stipulated that only the title of that particular novel could make it onto the screen. Indeed, he wouldn't even allow a paperback edition of the novel to be published in his lifetime (Fleming died in 1964).

In a bold effort to experiment with his tried and tested formula, the Bond creator had written his story from the perspective of a first-person narrator, a Vespa-riding Canadian woman named Vivienne Michel. This was especially risky, as female characters had never been Fleming's strong point, existing merely as objects for Bond to sleep with at the close of each adventure. In addition to being thinly written, they tended to spout appalling sentiments like "all women love semi-rape" (this specific line comes from Vivienne Michel and illustrates partly why her narrative met with such critical disdain). Another reason is that James Bond only appears very briefly, making a fortuitous arrival in the final act to rescue the imperilled heroine from two goons in an isolated motel (shades of *Psycho*). Consequently, Broccoli had no compunction about abandoning the story altogether when *The Spy Who Loved Me* began preproduction in March 1976.

The preceding Bond picture, *The Man with the Golden Gun* (1974), had received an unusually cool reception and, in 1975, a cash-strapped Saltzman sold his half of Eon Productions. *The Spy Who Loved Me* would, therefore, be the first entry that Broccoli would be producing alone. In essence, the future of the franchise relied on this pivotal film. As Broccoli told 'Screen International': "If it isn't [successful], we've had it, that's all…"

Knowing he would have to achieve something pretty spectacular to win back cinemagoers, Broccoli enlisted Lewis Gilbert, the director of the series' most outlandish entry up to that point, *You Only Live Twice* (1967). He also set a team of writers on initial screen treatments, including Anthony Burgess, a young John Landis, and the series' usual scripter Richard Maibaum. It was, however, Lewis Gilbert who hired the eventual screenwriter Christopher Wood.

Born in 1935, Wood was best known as Timothy Lea - the pseudonym under which he wrote the saucy 'Confessions' books and films. It was quite an unusual choice to bring the author of such madcap, low budget erotica into one of the glossiest franchises in movie history, especially when the very success of the series depended on his work. Imagine if the writer of, say, *Sex Lives of the Potato Men* (2004) had been chosen to script *Casino Royale* (2006).

Nevertheless, Wood improves vastly on Fleming's slight storyline, constructing a beautifully bonkers plot around a supervillain's desire to wipe out humankind and start a new underwater race. Initially, the criminal mastermind was to be Ernst Stavro Blofeld, head of Fleming's fictional crime organisation SPECTRE, but when producer Kevin McClory caught wind of this, he threatened legal action. (McClory had contributed story ideas to Fleming's 'Thunderball', the novel in which Blofeld and SPECTRE first appear). All references to SPECTRE were thus dropped and the villain became the amphibious Karl Stromberg (named after American TV producer Hunt Stromberg Jr, who helped to develop such classic titles as *The Twilight Zone, The Munsters* and *Lost in Space*). Stromberg is played, with a permanent scowl and webbed hands, by Austrian actor Curt Jürgens, who had previously worked with Lewis Gilbert on the 1959 actioner *Ferry to Hong Kong*.

Another refugee from that film, Milton Reid, was drafted in as one of Stromberg's henchmen, Sandor. Reid - who had played similar characters in *Dr No* (1962) and the spoof *Casino Royale* (1967) - bore a certain resemblance to Sluggsy, the totally hairless, moon-faced thug of Fleming's original novel.

But it was the second of the book's villains who would make a more inspired contribution: Horror, "a frightening lizard of a man", whose teeth are "cheaply capped with steel", became Stromberg's most chilling aide, the metal-toothed Jaws. Named, of course, after Spielberg's then-recent blockbuster, Jaws remains the most memorable Bond minion since Harold Sakata's Oddjob of *Goldfinger* (1964). He is played with a deft mix of mirth and menace by 7-foot-2 Richard Kiel, who had previously been the titular *Eegah* (1962), the cannibalistic alien in *The Twilight Zone* episode *To Serve Man* (1962), and Frankenstein's

Monster on *The Monkees* (1967).

It could be argued that the female perspective of Fleming's novel also found its way on screen in the stronger-than-usual characterisation of the Bond Girl, Anya Amasova. Our expectations of the typical leading lady in a 007 film are reversed right from the onset when it is revealed that Anya is a Soviet agent. Forced to work alongside Bond, she not only rises above 007's smarmy chauvinism, but also proves as adept as he is in taking on the baddies - that is, until the finale, when she finds herself bound in a skimpy outfit, waiting for Bond to rescue her. This was the 1970s, after all.

This climactic disappointment is countered by an earlier highlight in which Anya discovers Bond is responsible for the death of her lover (played by Michael Billington, who had screen-tested for the role of 007 more times than any other actor). The resultant scene, wherein Anya promises to kill Bond once their mission is over, is well conveyed by both actors. Moore, in particular, turns in his finest work in the series so far, proving he could be serious in the role (despite many objectors claiming his performances were too light-hearted).

It's worth noting that, throughout the '70s, a lighter approach to the character was insisted upon, not only by the filmmakers but also by the majority of cinemagoers who were living in a time of economic decline and social unrest. As an actor, Moore was merely responding to these demands. "People have enough problems in the world without going and seeing them on the screen," he explained to the BBC in an on-set interview. "It's better they should escape from the humdrum, normal existence into the world of fantasy, and relax. That's what entertainment means."

Parenthetically, the turn to a more humorous direction had actually begun with Connery's *Diamonds Are Forever* (1971) - which is kitschier than any of Roger's worst excesses.

One has only to look at Moore's performances as *The Saint* (1962-1969), *The Man Who Haunted Himself* (1970) or, indeed, his Bond of *For Your Eyes Only* (1981) to prove that he was more than capable of delivering the dramatic goods.

With *The Spy Who Loved Me*, the actor finally relaxes into the role, making it his own. He does, however, make one unfortunate thespic choice: Directly after the aforementioned scene between Bond and Anya, we cut to the pair being lowered aboard a nuclear submarine. While Barbara Bach's Anya is appropriately sullen, Moore is smirking at her in an annoyingly goading fashion, which only serves to undermine the sincerity of their previous exchange. Nevertheless, this is a small quibble; elsewhere, the chemistry between Moore and Bach is a sheer delight.

Bach - who had been slapped by *Thunderball*'s Claudine Auger in *Black Belly of the Tarantula* (1971) - would be

7

reunited with Richard Kiel on *Force 10 from Navarone* (1978) and *The Humanoid* (1979), before taking part in *Jaguar Lives!* (1979, a globe-hopping martial arts adventure which wastes other actors from the Bond franchise) and *Caveman* (1981), on which she met her husband Ringo Starr.

The rather clever introductory surprise of Anya's true status is followed by one of the most audacious stunts in cinema history: An exciting ski chase culminates in Bond plummeting from a 3,000-foot precipice, only to pull a Union Jack parachute at the final moment (the Leicester Square Odeon audience at the film's premiere was reportedly so bowled over by the feat that they burst into spontaneous applause).

This breath-taking jump was performed by Rick Sylvester, an out of work ski instructor, under the supervision of Olympic skier (and fashion designer) Willy Bogner Jr. Second unit director John Glen (who went on to helm all the '80s Eon Bond films) captured the action, which took place in July 1976 at Canada's Asgard Peak. Despite several camera crews being trained on Sylvester, only one camera caught the entirety of the stunt.

From this pre-titles sequence onwards, humour, glamour and spectacle assail us on a variety of exotic locations, all rendered by French cinematographer Claude Renoir in a painterly style worthy of his famed grandfather, Impressionist artist Pierre-Auguste Renoir.

Not only are successful elements from previous entries restaged with dazzling style (the ski chase of *On Her Majesty's Secret Service*, the train fight of *From Russia with Love*, the aquatic battles of *Thunderball*), there are also fun quotations from other movies (snatches of music from *Doctor Zhivago* and *Lawrence of Arabia* can be heard on the soundtrack).

But *The Spy Who Loved Me* is more than just a slick 'Greatest Hits' package. One modish touch sees Moore piloting the world's very first wetbike as he races to

save Anya. (Unfortunately, Moore's involvement in another stunt - his final duel with Stromberg - saw him nearly come a cropper, as he told the press: "I was blown out of the chair and had smouldering holes in my back").

Other modern elements include the Oscar-nominated production design of Ken Adam and Derek Meddings' brilliant miniature effects. Chief among their creations is Bond's submersible Lotus Esprit, which is pursued at high speed through the winding mountain roads of Sardinia (where principal photography began in September 1976). Among the pursuers is the nefarious helicopter pilot Naomi, played with relish by Hammer horror favourite Caroline Munro (of *Dracula AD 1972* and *Captain Kronos: Vampire Hunter*).

Munro's fellow Hammer alumna, Valerie Leon (*Blood from the Mummy's Tomb*) also appears in the Sardinia scenes, as the receptionist of the Hotel Cala di Volpe. (Leon would enjoy more screen-time alongside Connery's 007 in the unofficial entry *Never Say Never Again* in 1983).

Listen out, too, for the distinctive tones of Charles Gray (of Hammer's *The Devil Rides Out*), who makes an

uncredited third contribution to a Bond film (after *You Only Live Twice* and *Diamonds Are Forever*) as the narrator of the *son-et-lumière* pyramid attraction. Gray's vocal cameo takes place amid stunning Egyptian locations, where Cubby Broccoli displayed his magnanimous nature during a food shortage by singlehandedly cooking and serving spaghetti to the entire cast and crew. At the producer's memorial service in 1996, a tearful Lewis Gilbert described this as Cubby's finest hour.

Indeed, *The Spy Who Loved Me* proved in more ways than one that Broccoli could do it alone. With a budget of $13.5 million, his production was so lavish that an extra stage had to be built at Pinewood Studios to accommodate Stromberg's supertanker lair. Measuring 374 ft by 158 ft, with a maximum height of 50 ft, it was, up to that point, the largest soundstage in the world and is still the biggest in Europe.

Ken Adam, fresh from his Oscar-winning work on Stanley Kubrick's *Barry Lyndon* (1975), even requested Kubrick's advice on how to light the massive set. (Kubrick's daughter, Katharina, was already working on the film, having designed Richard Kiel's steel teeth). Taking seven months to construct, the now famous 007 Stage was officially opened at a star-studded ceremony on 5th December 1976 by the former Prime Minister Harold Wilson.

Three months after shooting wrapped in January 1977, composer Marvin Hamlisch recorded his score, which remains the best in the series *not* to be composed by John Barry. As well as Carly Simon's Oscar-nominated theme song, *Nobody Does It Better* (a Top 10 hit on both sides of the Atlantic), Hamlisch delivers an enjoyably melodic soundtrack, inspired in part by the pulsating rhythms of the Bee Gees' contemporary output.

While listening to the accompanying LP, fans could also read Christopher Wood's novelisation. Despite some cringy sexist prose, the book provides backstories for the villains and additional gruesome details. At one point, Bond even has his testicles electrified!

Upon its release in July 1977, *The Spy Who Loved Me* was one of the biggest grossing movies of the year, an especially commendable feat given the parlous state of the British film industry at that time. Just above it in the Top 10 were *Star Wars* and *Close Encounters of the Third Kind* - two films which would influence the course of Roger Moore's next Bond outing *Moonraker*.

But that's another story…

Stephen Mooley is the author of 'Christopher Lee: The Loneliness of Evil' (Midnight Marquee Press).

# When Disaster Movies Ruled the World:
## Surviving a Decade of Cinematic Mass Destruction

by John Harrison

Whether people-made or an unkind act of nature, a disaster - or the ominous threat of it - has always proven a popular subject for filmmakers to dramatize or exploit. The bigger the looming cataclysm, the more exciting and tense the drama. In much the same way as we stay glued to news channels and websites whenever some big terrorist attack, earthquake or tsunami unfolds, we become intrigued by the grand humanity of the event, thankful we are far from it, yet also putting ourselves in the same situation, wondering how we would react in the face of such mad, mass panic.

Disasters, of both fact and fiction, had hit movie screens countless times prior to the '70s, whether in the form of a giant rogue star slamming into Earth in George Pal's special effects tour de force *When Worlds Collide* (1951), a passenger plane soaring through the skies without a pilot in *Zero Hour!* (1957) or the depiction of the mighty *Titanic* sinking to the bottom of the icy Atlantic on its maiden voyage in *A Night to Remember* (1958). However, there is no doubt that the '70s was the decade in which the disaster film was at its most popular and genre-defining. Indeed, the decade kicked off with the biggest disaster imaginable, as Earth was burned to a cinder at the cataclysmic finale of *Beneath the Planet of the Apes* (1970, see 'Cinema of the '70s' #4). But the birth of the modern disaster film is widely - and rightly - regarded to be George Seaton's *Airport* (1970). Released in March 1970, *Airport* was based on the novel of the same name by British/Canadian writer Arthur Hailey, first published in 1968 by Doubleday.

'The Master of Disaster'. Allen was already an established and well-known figure to fantasy film fans, mostly as the creator and producer of a quartet of classic science-fiction and fantasy television shows of the '60s: *Voyage to the Bottom of the Sea* (1964-68), *Lost in Space* (1965-68), *The Time Tunnel* (1966-67) and *Land of the Giants* (1968-70). His knowledge and first-hand experience working with miniatures and other special effects on those shows no doubt gave him confidence when he turned his attention to putting *The Poseidon Adventure* (1972) onto the big screen for 20th Century Fox. Based on a pulpy 1969 adventure novel by Paul Gallico, *The Poseidon Adventure* was more fast-paced and rousing than *Airport*. Directed by respected Englishman Ronald Neame, the plot of *The Poseidon Adventure* is centred around the titular aged luxury liner, the *SS Poseidon*, on her final journey from New York to Athens and the scrapyard. As the *Poseidon*'s final haul of passengers celebrate New Year's Eve, an enormous wave, triggered by an underwater earthquake, overturns the ocean liner, leaving a small band of survivors trapped inside below the waterline. Led by Frank Scott, a radical young reverend played by Gene Hackman, the group attempt to make their way up to the bottom of the *Poseidon*, in the chance that a part of the hull will still be

Universal Pictures hired writer/director Seaton to turn Hailey's book into a filmable screenplay, cramming it with a roll call of stars that included Burt Lancaster, Dean Martin, George Kennedy, Van Heflin, Jean Seberg, Jacqueline Bisset, Helen Hayes and more. It set a casting template for the disaster epics to follow: topline it with a couple of big names who are still near the peak of their star power, then fill the supporting cast with a group of fading stars for the nostalgia crowd and a few young up-and-comers to appeal to the all-important youth audience.

Despite its leisurely pace and soap opera-heavy plot (the disaster/thriller elements coming mostly in the form of a bomb threat aboard a Boeing 707), *Airport* proved a huge crowd-pleaser, taking in over $100 million at the American box-office. Though Lancaster famously dismissed it as "the biggest piece of junk ever made", it was nominated for ten Academy Awards, including Best Picture, Best Writing (Adapted Screenplay), Best Cinematography and Best Original Score. It eventually ended up winning only one (Hayes for Best Supporting Actress), but proved that a big-scale disaster movie could bring both financial success and prestige to a studio.

It was then that Irwin Allen would enter the picture and soon make the disaster genre his own, becoming so synonymous with it that he would forever be known as

featuring enjoyable (if over the top) performances from most of the cast. Launched with an aggressive marketing campaign, the film became an enormous box-office hit when it was released in December 1972, helped along by the theme song *The Morning After*, which in the movie was sung by Renne Armand (providing a vocal double for Lynley) but became a chart success when recorded by Maureen McGovern and released as a single in 1973.

Building on the success of *The Poseidon Adventure*, the disaster film would hit its peak in 1974, with the release of three big studio pictures: *Earthquake, The Towering Inferno* and *Airport '75* (which, despite its title, was released in October 1974). Depicting the lead-up to a massive quake which causes catastrophic damage to the majority of Los Angeles, as well as the struggle for survival in the face of its aftermath, *Earthquake* had perhaps the most ludicrous casting of all the big '70s disaster movies, with Lorne Greene playing Ava Gardner's father, despite the fact that Greene was only seven years older than her! Gardner, playing the jealous and bitter wife of former football star Charlton Heston, puts in a hysterical and overly dramatic performance, running to daddy and faking overdoses in order to get attention and her way, but the rest of *Earthquake*'s cast is equally quirky and fun.

above the surface and a rescue team will be awaiting them. Among those joining him on his treacherous adventure are Ernest Borgnine and Stella Stevens (as a gruff ex-cop and his one-time hooker wife), Roddy McDowall (as the ship's dining room attendant), Shelley Winters and Jack Albertson (as a retired couple heading to Israel to meet their small grandson for the first time), Pamela Sue Martin (as a teenager stuck with her bratty, know-it-all younger brother) and Carol Lynley as the *Poseidon*'s young lounge singer. Partly filmed aboard the *RMS Queen Mary* (whose encounter with a near-hundred-foot rogue wave in December 1942 provided the initial inspiration for Gallico's novel), *The Poseidon Adventure* has a near-perfect balance of exaggerated melodrama and exciting peril, punctuated by still-impressive stunts and set-pieces, and

There's Shaft himself, Richard Roundtree, as a struggling Evel Knievel wannabe in tight black leathers with bright orange lightning bolts (he looks like a blaxploitation riff on the classic Spiderman villain Electro). There's also Marjoe Gortner as a grocery store manager-cum-National Guard reservist, with a psychotic and perverted edge that suited the preacher-turned-actor's look and demeanour perfectly. Co-written by 'The Godfather' scribe Mario Puzo, and directed by Mark Robson, the special effects in *Earthquake* range from very impressive to laughably ludicrous. Animated drops of blood flying at the camera (during the scene when a packed elevator crashes to the

ground) and an obvious lens distortion trick to depict city buildings swaying in the quake would have seemed ineffective even at the time, but on the other hand, there is some terrific miniature and model work on display, particularly in the destruction of the Mulholland Dam and the subsequent flooding.

The biggest special effect in *Earthquake*, however, was not visual but aural. To enhance the experience for the audience, Universal Studios and loudspeaker manufacturer Cerwin-Vega combined to create Sensurround, a new sound system featuring a low frequency noise generator that added simulated rumbles and vibrations to the movie, effectively rattling the audience in their seats during the earthquake sequences. Costing $2,000 to install in each cinema that wanted to use the process, Sensurround was certainly effective as a cinematic gimmick (in the vein of 3D in the '50s) and an enormous benefit to the marketing campaign for *Earthquake*, yet the process failed to really take-off, and was used by Universal in only three other films: *Midway* (1976), *Rollercoaster* (1977, see 'Cinema of the '70s' #3) and the pilot episode of *Battlestar Galactica* (1979), which was released theatrically in many countries.

Directed by John Guillermin and once again produced

with much ballyhoo by Irwin Allen, *The Towering Inferno* is perhaps the ultimate example of the '70s disaster movie. The project was so enormous, it took the combined financial strength of 20th Century Fox and Warner Brothers to realize it (the first such joint venture between two major Hollywood studios). The story was sourced from two different novels: Richard Martin Stern's 'The Tower' (1973) and 'The Glass Inferno' (1974) by Thomas N. Scortia and Frank M. Robinson (confusion was no doubt created when both novels were subsequently reprinted as official film tie-in paperback editions). Paul Newman and Steve McQueen demanded and received equal pay, equal top billing and, so the story goes, an equal number of lines of dialogue. Cast as the architect and the fire chief respectively, Newman and McQueen's characters are brought together when cheap wiring sparks a fire inside the world's tallest building, the 138-storey Glass Tower in San Francisco, on its opening night! Not the sort of publicity the building's owner (William Holden) wants, so he tries to keep the fire quiet from his high-profile guests, who are partying away in the Promenade Room on the 135th floor while the blaze starts spreading fifty floors beneath them. Soon everyone is trapped inside the Glass Tower, as stairwells explode and become blocked, elevators short circuit in the heat and die, and all other means of escape slowly become cut-off from the diminishing band of survivors, and people become more desperate and cut-throat in their desperation to stay alive. Re-watching *The Towering Inferno* today, it's hard not to let your head fill with haunting memories of 9/11, those harrowing images that were forever seared into our minds that day, news footage repeated over and over of the Twin Towers engulfed in flames and black smoke, and some occupants inside choosing to leap to their deaths rather than be burned or suffer the horror of smoke inhalation.

Aside from its huge commercial success, *The Towering Inferno* was also well-received critically, earning eight Oscar nominations, including Best Picture, and ultimately winning three of them (for Best Cinematography, Best Film Editing and Best Original Song). Despite its many genuinely impressive highlights, *The Towering Inferno* is not as tight a film as *The Poseidon Adventure*, which Allen was clearly trying his best to surpass in every way. But the sheer scale of the production cannot help but impress, especially considering how much real controlled fire was used on the set and how it all could have easily gotten out of hand.

In *Airport '75*, Universal brought back Charlton Heston from *Earthquake* and made a much more tense and exciting film than the original *Airport*, bringing the concept in line with what the recent disaster films had done so successfully. With his usual machismo, Heston plays Captain Alan Murdock, a pilot and flight instructor dating chief stewardess Nancy Pryor (Karen Black) but not

"Something hit us... the crew is dead... help us, please, please help us!"

**NEW** Screen excitement—
inspired by the novel "AIRPORT" by Arthur Hailey.

# AIRPORT 1975

CHARLTON HESTON

KAREN BLACK · GEORGE KENNEDY · GLORIA SWANSON · EFREM ZIMBALIST JR. · SUSAN CLARK · SID CAESAR · LINDA BLAIR
DANA ANDREWS · ROY THINNES · NANCY OLSON · ED NELSON · NORMA VARDEN · AUGUSTA SUMMERLAND and HELEN REDDY

Written by DON INGALLS · Directed by JACK SMIGHT · Music by JOHN CACAVAS · Produced by WILLIAM FRYE · Executive Producer JENNINGS LANG
A UNIVERSAL PICTURE · TECHNICOLOR® · PANAVISION®

**PG** PARENTAL GUIDANCE SUGGESTED

wanting to commit to her. Pryor is flying to Los Angeles on a massive Boeing 747 when the pilot of a small private plane suffers a heart attack and flies his aircraft straight into the 747, destroying half the cockpit and killing most of its flight crew, apart from Captain Stacy (Efrem Zimbalist, Jr.), who is blinded and severely injured in the collision, leaving him in no shape to pilot the plane. With an Air Traffic Control crew on the ground broadcasting instructions through the radio, it is up to Nancy to keep the crippled jumbo in the air, avoiding treacherous mountain ranges until Murdock can get himself aboard via a precarious mid-air transfer from a Sikorsky helicopter, a sequence which is impressively staged and filled with genuine suspense. Naturally, there is still a lot of exposition, hysterics and personal dramas running throughout *Airport '75*, all ably provided by another diverse gathering of faces. Linda Blair plays the teenager en route to a life-saving kidney transplant, Australian singer Helen Reddy the nun who soothes her with tunes on her acoustic guitar. Sid Caesar, Norman Fell and Jerry Stiller provide the bad sit-com level humour, delivering lines that would have even made old vaudeville audiences groan. But best of all is Gloria Swanson, the famous silent film star who brilliantly played on her past in Billy Wilder's classic noir drama *Sunset Boulevard* (1950). Here she drops all pretence at playing a character and is simply credited as playing herself, returning to LA with her assistant to deliver her precious memoirs to the publisher. Supposedly, Swanson wrote all her own dialogue, and it results in a strange kind of juxtaposition between the old-Hollywood glamor of the silent era, and the grand but mostly vapid spectacle of the then-modern blockbuster.

*Airport '75* also benefits from a terrific performance from the late Karen Black, probably one of the few really strong and demanding female roles in a disaster film from that period. Statuesque and one of the uniquely beautiful and quintessential faces of '70s American cinema, Black puts her character through a wide range of emotions, from sheer terror to frustration and resignation to grim determination, and it's fair to say that she holds the film together in a dramatical sense, and is a much more important and sympathetic, not to mention more easily identifiable, character than Heston's. George Kennedy reprises his role of Joe Patroni, a tradition he would repeat for the two further *Airport* sequels, becoming not just one of the regular faces of disaster cinema, but providing the only identifiable actor and character to link the *Airport* series together.

1977 saw the third of the *Airport* films released, the cleverly titled *Airport '77* (1977), which is my personal favourite of the series, achieving a terrific balance of eclectic casting and a plot that is outlandish yet effectively

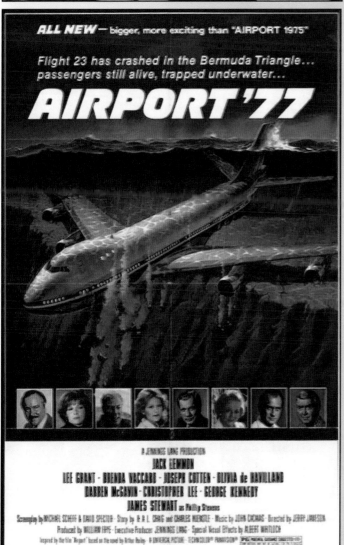

engrossing. Directed by Jerry Jameson - having come a long way from *The Bat People* (1974) - *Airport '77* throws a heist element into the mix, as a privately-owned 747 carrying priceless works of art is hijacked mid-air, with the caper going awry and the plane plummeting into the middle of the Bermuda Triangle and sinking intact into the ocean! Resting precariously on an underwater shelf, just above crush level but too deep to open the doors and swim to the surface, the surviving passengers are trapped not knowing if the plane's direction was even being tracked after the hijacking attempt. This gives our cast of characters time to work out their phobias and angst with each other, none more so than Lee Grant, who puts in a classic bitchy and boozy performance as the bored wife of Christopher Lee, who in a nice turn of events gets to play a more heroic role than what we were used to seeing him in at the time.

By the late '70s, the disaster film looked to have peaked, though no one could tell Irwin Allen, who gathered another big-name ensemble to tackle an invasion of deadly killer African bees in *The Swarm* (1978). While melodrama was a big part of the disaster genre, *The Swarm* is so over-the-top yet played so deadly serious by the cast, it almost becomes a parody of itself. Michael Caine, top-billed as an entomologist who is tracking the migration of the bees as they make their destructive way up through Texas, barks his lines as if they are military orders, and does it with a completely straight face. Caine is certainly not helped by those around him (an ensemble which includes

Katharine Ross, Richard Widmark, Olivia de Havilland, Cameron Mitchell, Fred MacMurray and Patty Duke), nor by the terrible screenplay by Stirling Silliphant. Unlike his previous big disaster hits, where Allen directed the action sequences but handed over the drama to a more seasoned director, in *The Swarm* he decided to handle all the direction himself, which was possibly a money-saving decision but certainly the wrong one, as he doesn't seem to handle an all-star cast as well as he directs the flipping of an ocean liner or the burning of a skyscraper. Though *The Swarm* signalled the start of the decline of the '70s

disaster film genre (it was not only critically ridiculed but bombed commercially), it is still a lot of fun and rarely boring. My favourite moments are when a bratty kid and his two friends throw Molotov cocktails at the giant beehive in a park and then take cover under garbage cans, the sight of de Havilland looking on in horror as small kids are stung to death in a schoolyard (in slow-motion, no less), the hilarious giant bee hallucinations that some of the survivors of their sting experience, and the bee attack on the mountain train, which provides one of the film's genuinely impressive highlights (and in which Allen finds the perfect way to solve a love triangle between three

18

mature age singles).

Allen was back, and once again in the director's chair, the following year with his long-promised *Beyond the Poseidon Adventure* (1979). Michael Caine and Telly Savalas both arrive to salvage the *Poseidon* the day after it capsized. Caine is looking for gold, jewellery and money, Savalas for weapons and plutonium (it is never really explained what such a deadly cargo was doing aboard a luxury passenger liner). They stumble upon some surviving passengers still trapped inside the hull of the doomed ship, and have to face off against each other and the dangers present as they seek to find a way back to the surface after their exit route becomes blocked. Lacking the tightness and terrific ensemble that made *The Poseidon Adventure* such an effective and tense adventure/thriller, *Beyond the Poseidon Adventure* still has a sense of late '70s fun and the usual disaster film roll call of stars young and old, including Karl Malden, Shirley Jones, Angela Cartwright, Sally Field, Slim Pickens and Peter Boyle, the latter almost channelling his notorious racist character from *Joe* (1970).

A co-production between American International Pictures (AIP) and the Shaw Brothers of Hong Kong, *Meteor* (1979) hoped to catch the tail end of the disaster movie cycle as well as ride the wave of science-fiction adventure cinema, which was then at a phenomenal level of popularity, thanks of course to *Star Wars* (1977) and *Close Encounters of the Third Kind* (1977). In *Meteor*, the United States and the Soviet Union are forced to admit the existence of outer space weaponry, after a comet collides with an asteroid belt, sending a huge five-mile chunk of rock dubbed Orpheus, as well as several smaller fragments, hurtling straight towards Earth. Fortunately, both the USA and the USSR have developed satellites bearing nuclear missiles to orbit the Earth in readiness for just such an occasion. Unfortunately, political and military pressure in both countries have resulted in the missiles pointing inwards, towards their Earth-based enemies, rather than outwards towards their intergalactic ones. Sean Connery plays the NASA scientist who helped design the American satellite, but walked away when he discovered it was going to be used for military purposes. Returning to the space agency only out of humanity's necessity, Bradley has to knock brains with his Russian counterpart (Brian Keith) to find a way to remotely re-direct both of the satellites and fire their weapons at the right time so that the combined firepower will hit the largest of the threatening asteroids at the same time.

Produced at a time when the military potential of outer space was being seriously investigated (culminating in President Ronald Reagan's infamous 'Star Wars' program in the early '80s), *Meteor* has lots of Cold War angst and tension, embodied primarily in the character of General Adlon (Martin Landau), who is extremely incensed and distrustful of allowing the Russians into their secret New

York underground bunker, from where the American satellite is operated. Romance is present in the form of Natalie Wood as Tatiana Donskaya, the Russian interpreter who accompanies Keith's character to the US, and immediately catches the eye of Connery. Bringing in *The Poseidon Adventure*'s Ronald Neame as director may have seemed like a natural recipe for success, but unfortunately *Meteor* had little of the genuine suspense and excitement of his earlier hit, and it became one of the final gasps in the big-budget disaster movie cycle from that period. While the special effects here are less than stellar, using unconvincing

miniatures and matte paintings, the New York sequence is memorable in its way for showing the destruction of the Twin Towers of the World Trade Centre, an image which (as discussed previously) will now always appear more startling and evocative then ever intended.

Despite a big promotional and merchandising campaign (which spawned everything from a comic book adaptation, to a Viewmaster set, and even a pinball machine), *Meteor* proved to be a financial bust at the box-office, a failure which led to the eventual collapse of AIP and indicated that audience interest in disaster epics was clearly on the wane.

1979 also bought us the final instalment in the *Airport* series, with *The Concorde… Airport '79* (or *Airport '80: The Concorde*, as it was released as in many international markets the following year). First flown in 1969 and entering service seven years later, *Airport '79* arrived perhaps a year or two too late to really capitalize on the hype and excitement generated by the sleek and futuristic new commercial passenger jet. After all, technology was progressing rapidly and the inaugural space shuttle flight was only two years away. It reportedly took producer Jennings Lang a few years to finally get permission to use the

Concorde from Air France, so it was obviously something they were hoping to exploit a lot earlier. Unfortunately, the majestic plane was hardly given the showcase it deserved in this ludicrous tale of a corrupt arms dealer (Robert Wagner) who uses everything from heat-seeking missiles to an F-4 Phantom jet to try and down an American Concorde on its maiden flight, after he discovers a female reporter (Susan Blakely) is aboard with papers that prove he has been providing weapons to communist countries. In a genre that was already balancing precariously on the edge, *The Concorde…Airport '79* really pushed things further towards self-parody and satire. Director David Lowell Rich seems totally disinterested in creating any genuine tension or drama, going for completely unrealistic mid-air action scenes made even less effective by sub-par special photographic effects (though the miniature of the Concorde itself is pretty good). The supporting cast is one of the most eclectic in the series and includes brooding French heartthrob Alain Delon, soft porn queen Sylvia Kristel, Spanish-born television personality Charo, Sybil Danning and Jimmie Walker.

Released not long after *Airport '79* was Jim Abrahams' and David and Jerry Zucker's classic comedy spoof *Airplane!* (1980), which sent up the *Airport* films in juvenile and often tasteless but brilliant and hilarious style (although the main narrative drive of the film was actually lifted from *Zero Hour!*). A surprise hit, *Airplane!* quickly tapped into a pop culture zeitgeist, with many of the gags in the film becoming a part of our everyday lexicon ("I am serious, and don't call me Shirley!") Leslie Nielsen reinvented himself as a deadpan comedy performer, an image he rode out for the remainder of both his career and his life, and *Airplane!* stuck the boot in so well that it's now impossible to watch *Zero Hour!* or any of the *Airport* films without immediately spotting specific scenes later signalled out for satire in *Airplane!* and openly chuckling to yourself because of it. No big disaster movie released in the immediate wake of *Airplane!* was likely to be taken seriously. It announced a timely and a strangely fitting end to the great disaster film cycle of the '70s.

# THE BIG BUS

**by Peter Sawford**

Comedy as a film genre has changed dramatically over the years. Writers and comedians love to push the envelope, to test the limit of what's allowable at the time, and often find themselves fighting the constraints of the prevailing production code.

In the silent era, slapstick was king. But the arrival of sound saw screwball comedies, with their fast pacing and even faster dialogue, come to the fore where they reigned supreme throughout the '30s and '40s. The late '40s and early '50s saw the rise of the Ealing comedies, and the '60s brought the seaside postcard humour of the Carry On series. There was also a darker style of comedy which poked fun at the problems of the world, including the possibility of impending nuclear holocaust.

The '70s - despite the turmoil of the Vietnam War, Watergate and international terrorism - saw the dawn of a more flippant and irreverent style: the spoof film.

In the vanguard of this new sub-genre was Mel Brooks. In a few short years, he spoofed everything from westerns (*Blazing Saddles*, 1974) to horror (*Young Frankenstein*, 1974), from the silent era (*Silent Movie*, 1976) to Hitchcock (*High Anxiety*, 1977).

Brooks would stay at the top of the pile into the early '80, but in 1976 a film was released which, while not quite enough to depose Brooks from his lofty perch, at least made him look over his shoulder with genuine concern. *The Big Bus* was a parody of the disaster movies so prevalent at the time. Despite doing more to set the template for future spoofs than possibly any other film, it has been largely forgotten and unfairly neglected.

The big bus in question is *Cyclops*, the world's first nuclear-powered, double-decked, articulated bus, capable of driving non-stop from New York to Denver.

Designed to revolutionise cross-country bus travel, it has everything from a lounge bar with resident piano player to a ten-pin bowling alley and a swimming pool. But a sinister super criminal caged in an iron lung is determined to sabotage it at all costs to appease his oil-producing paymasters.

An explosion at the bus depot, masterminded by Ironman (Jose Ferrer) and executed by his brother Alex (Stuart Margolin) days before *Cyclops* is due to start its maiden trip, badly injures the two crew members due to drive the bus. Professor Baxter (Harold Gould), the designer of *Cyclops*, is also hurt in the blast.

With the date scheduled for *Cyclops*' maiden journey fast approaching, Baxter's daughter Kitty (Stockard Channing) is given the job of finding a replacement crew and turns to

disgraced bus driver and ex-fiancé, Dan Torrance (Joseph Bologna). Torrance is vilified by all the other bus drivers after being accused of eating passengers to stay alive when a previous bus he was driving crashed on Mount Diablo. Torrance claims to have eaten the luggage and coach seats as per his training and had only eaten a foot that had been put in a stew without his knowledge. But his protestations are in vain, and he remains an outcast amongst those he used to call friends.

Chosen to assist Torrance is Shoulders O'Brien (John Beck), a square-jawed, heroic-looking sidekick who aides Torrance in a vicious barroom brawl ("look out, he's got a broken milk carton"), but hides a worrying medical condition.

The passengers on this first journey are a disparate group, each battling their own problems and inner demons. Dr. Kurtz (Bob Dishy) is a disgraced vet looking for redemption and a chance to get his practising licence back. His veterinarian training proves useful when he treats the injured passengers. Then there's Emery Bush (Richard B. Shull), a man who has only six months to live and wants to see the seven wonders of the world while he still can. He's had a somewhat blasé approach since his diagnosis but discovers that his grip on life is still as tight as ever when the chance of a heroic death is offered him. Camille Levy (Lynn Redgrave) is a nymphomaniac socialite who has a don't-give-a-damn attitude and a secretly craves revenge on the man who ate the owner of the wing tip shoe she carries around. Ruth Gordon plays a role similar to her later character in *Every Which Way but Loose* and *Any Which Way You Can*, a cantankerous octogenarian running away from home for the first time. She has the bad luck to find herself seated next to Father Kudos (Rene Auberjonois), a priest who has lost his faith and openly mocks anyone who still has even a shred of belief.

The real stars of the passenger list however are Sybil and Claude Crane (Sally Kellerman and Richard Mulligan), a warring, soon-to-be-divorced couple who scream and shout at each other, trading barbed comments and vicious insults one minute, while making passionate love in the

nearest (and often most inappropriate) spot the next.

Back at the depot, Shorty Scotty (Ned Beatty) and Jack (Howard Hesseman) oversee the logistics of the journey while struggling to monitor the computer systems, the numerous untested options on *Cyclops* and their own complicated relationship.

Although based on the disaster movies so prevalent in the early '70s, the writers expand their boundaries to parody a number of other genres as well.

Ironman and his dim brother Alex are a master criminal and sidekick in the best tradition of Goldfinger & Oddjob or Scaramanga & Nick Nack. Their plans mirror anything the great 007 villains could dream up. Sadly for Ironman, Alex is as much a hindrance to him as a help.

When Kitty finds Dan, he's visiting his father's grave looking for answers. The meeting has all the hallmarks of a '40s film noir, with tightly buckled trenchcoats, smooth trumpet music in the background and a conversation which drips with double meanings. Cheesy Douglas Sirk potboilers, gritty '40s action films, '70s sci-fi television and lurid '60s pop culture are all aped and spoofed, while *The Italian Job* is raided for the cliff-hanger episode near the end as the big bus teeters on the brink, leaving its passengers and crew with no option but to flood the rear compartment with soft drinks (Channing recounted how she nearly drowned for real while filming this sequence).

When I first saw *The Big Bus*, I thought it was another of the *Airplane!* knock offs made in the wake of the Zucker Brothers' creation. Only later did I find out it was actually made four years before, and stands as more of a template for *Airplane!* than anything Brooks ever did.

It's not just its sense of cross-genre comedy, it's also the straight-arrow delivery of lines. All the Mel Brooks films felt like they knew they were comedies and so did everyone in them, but *The Big Bus* is intentionally played as if it's deadly serious. Bologna acts like he genuinely believes he's the heroic driver of an experimental bus; Channing's description of how to put on the Haz-mat suits in case the reactor leaks, and what symptoms to look out for if people don't get the suits on quickly enough, is a masterclass of deadpan comic delivery worthy of Leslie Nielsen at his best.

*The Big Bus* even preceded *Airplane!*'s technique of having a single running gag the length of the film. In *Airplane!* the jet engines are dubbed with the sound of a propeller driven plane. In *The Big Bus*, Kitty is told her father can't be moved from the car park by the Doctor (Larry Hagman) and asked to sign a waiver absolving him of all responsibility if anything goes wrong. "But you're a Doctor!" Kitty cries. "And I intend to remain one!" the Doctor solemnly replies, as gradually a whole ward grows around her father in the bus depot car park, complete with screens, heart monitors, oxygen tanks, intravenous tubes and ventilators.

The bus itself more than passes muster as a believable

mode of transport with its automatic tyre changing and window washing systems. It was created by the simple process of bolting two buses together, but was still capable of driving from Los Angeles to San Diego to promote the film.

The Big Bus was released by Paramount Pictures on 23rd June, 1976, and came from the creative minds of director James Frawley and writer/producers Fred Freeman and Lawrence J. Cohen. They had all previously worked in American television, on programmes like *Columbo*, *Gilligan's Island*, *Bewitched* and *The Andy Griffiths Show*.

Sadly, the trio never got to work again on a film. They weren't approached by Paramount or any other studios to reunite. I think this is sad, as they show an excellent feel for the genre and could have created another spoof classic.

David Shire's opening music and various themes throughout superbly capture the prevailing style of the more serious disaster films of the time, much like Elmer Bernstein's hilarious score for *Airplane!*

On release the film got moderate to poor reviews from critics but gained a devoted group of supporters. It played in cinemas briefly, made just over $3.5m, then disappeared as if it had never been made.

Over the years, it's gained the epithet that many films deemed a flop on release end up with - the tag of cult classic. Sadly, unlike many other cult classics, *The Big Bus* appears to have been forgotten by the good men and women who control the television schedules. It never seems to turn up any more, not even in late night or early morning slots, nor even as a Sunday afternoon antidote to football, cricket or motor racing.

Like many other cult classics, *The Big Bus* enjoyed a revival during the video boom of the early '80s. People were hungry for more of the same after watching *Airplane!*, and found *The Big Bus* in the same section at the rental store. This revival, however, proved as short-lived as its initial theatrical release.

The entire cast went on to bigger, and in some cases better, things in the following years. Bologna, *The Big Bus*'s archetypal action hero, went on to appear in films such as *My Favourite Year*, *Blame it on Rio* and *The Woman in Red* and was busy right up to his death from cancer in 2017. Feisty and sexy Channing appeared in her signature role as Betty Rizzo in *Grease* two years later, and has been seen regularly on both the big screen and television ever since (one of her best known roles is that of First Lady Abbey Bartlett in *The West Wing*). Hagman probably made the biggest jump, from car park doctor to power-mad oil baron J.R. Ewing in *Dallas* two years later. He was joined in that TV behemoth for a short time by John Beck (minus the narcolepsy). Murphy Dunne got a role in *The Blues Brothers* because John Landis had seen his turn in *The Big Bus* as the cheesy lounge room singer. Mulligan went on to star in the hugely successful US sitcoms *Soap* and *Empty Nest*. Auberjoinois appeared in numerous films, including the dodgy remake of *King Kong* (1977) and *Police Academy 5* (1988). Kellerman remained busy and in-demand into her eighties, and passed away only last year.

As with many great comedy films, *The Big Bus* needs multiple viewings as so many funny lines and moments can be missed while you're still laughing at the last joke. Is it as good as *Airplane!*? No, not in my opinion. It's certainly a sort of prototype for that film, but it can't match the sheer number of jokes per minute that *Airplane!* achieved. And though I love *The Big Bus*, I have to admit a few of its gags fall flat and it sags slightly in the middle. The somewhat shuddering ending suggests the writers couldn't fully make up their minds how to finish things. Putting those quibbles aside, I urge anybody who hasn't seen it yet to put that right. It's still available on DVD and I guarantee that by catching catch *The Big Bus*, you'll be taken on a journey you won't forget or regret.

# SORCERER

by Darren Linder

Director William Friedkin considers *Sorcerer* (1977) his greatest film, and who are we to disagree with the master? Unfortunately, it bombed at the box office and was not readily available in a decent print for decades. Only recently has the remastered, untampered-with version been made available, and it truly secures the film's place as one of the greatest of the '70s. I was lucky enough to attend a theatrical screening of the digital restoration of *Sorcerer*, and I count it among the greatest cinematic experiences of my life. Friedkin became a household name and a New Hollywood player by winning the Best Director and Best Film Academy Awards for his 1971 crime film *The French Connection*. His next gig was directing what became an international pop-culture phenomenon and arguably the greatest horror movie ever made, *The Exorcist* (1973). Both films were successful in part due to Friedkin's background in making documentaries in the '60s. The realism he brought to both *The French Connection* and *The Exorcist* was a huge reason for their success. Who can forget that frenetic chase in *The French Connection*, for example, between Gene Hackman in a car and the villain on an elevated train? This was filmed guerrilla style without obtaining permits or having the streets controlled at all. Those weren't stunt drivers in the other cars; they were regular civilians completely unaware that a movie was being filmed. A real crash which occurred appears in this chase

sequence. And, as disturbing as many scenes are in *The Exorcist*, one of the most unnerving moments is watching twelve-year-old Regan undergoing a spinal tap procedure and brain scan. The intense sound of the huge scanning machine doing the pneumoencephalogram, needles puncturing her skin and arterial blood spurts make this almost more horrific than the head-spinning and crucifix masturbation scenes. Amidst dozens of graphic moments of demonic possession, how telling it is that the scene which haunts people is that harrowing medical procedure. Friedkin's documentary background has much to do with the success of these scenes, and these films.

After the massive success of these two early '70s films, Friedkin was essentially issued a blank check for his next project. With it, he decided to do a remake (or, to use his word, a "reimagining") of the 1953 French film *Le salaire de la peur* (aka *The Wages of Fear*). The basic story is that several down-on-their-luck men take a mission to transport explosives to a remote mining rig deep in the South American jungle. The explosives will be used to put out a huge oil well fire if they can get them there safely. But the dynamite is unstable and the nitroglycerin is leaking out, meaning that any large bump or drop could cause it to explode. The four men drive in two trucks, traveling over unmaintained roads and rickety bridges. This simple premise sets up a new classic along the lines of *Treasure of the Sierra Madre,* where the 'Making Of' story reminds me of *Fitzcarraldo.*

Friedkin took his production all over the world, filming in France, Mexico, Israel, the Dominican Republic and the United States. Location filming is essential for this kind of story, but it invariably ends up using a lot of the budget and there's always the risk of being plagued with unforeseen weather disasters. The budget ballooned from $15 million to $22 million, and the real-life behind-the-scenes story is almost as intense as the film itself. *Sorcerer* shares similar production struggles with Werner Herzog's *Aguirre, the Wrath of God* (1972) and my favorite film, Francis Ford Coppola's *Apocalypse Now* (1979). All three explore obsession, insanity and megalomania, and suggest that if you travel too deep into the primal jungle, you will

not return the same (if you return at all).

Another way Friedkin elevates *Sorcerer* is by adding small touches that I call 'visual poetry.' None of these shots do anything to further the story, and some editors would remove them to save time, but they're vital because they put us directly there in that town, in that moment, and add humanity and realness to the scenes. Perhaps also stemming from his documentary background, these little moments of beauty juxtaposed with the muck and death make the film a masterpiece. Sometimes it's just an unusual detail, like an officer pulling back the slide of his .45, not because he's chambering a round to menace someone but because he's using the pistol's edge as a bottle opener to open his Coca-Cola. Friedkin spends time showing us creatures living amongst the detritus of the desperately poor town. A man lays passed out in the mud, while crabs crawl across garbage, combing through it for anything edible. A naked boy walks out of a dilapidated shack, reminiscent of a scene in Jodorowsky's 1970 film *El Topo.*

Dogs eat scraps out of the debris-strewn mud street. A bartender sprays insecticide from an old-fashioned pump bug spray right onto the bar inches away from a patron who is passed out. That same bartender brings out food and, almost as an afterthought, cleans the utensils by simply wiping them on his sweat-drenched shirt. A butterfly is shown perched on some chicken wire fencing. An official receives bribe money and pulls it toward him with a fly swatter. Lots of insectoid imagery, carrion eaters and abject poverty and alcoholism are shown.

More visual poetry is found in the set dressing. There is a scene involving the main characters landing by plane on a dirt airstrip. This is the dirtiest plane you've ever seen, and the husk of another plane still lies on the side of the runway. The implication is that a plane crashed and exploded long ago, and the frame was simply left there like roadkill on a highway shoulder. When they get to the nearby town, the bustling street life is rich and believable. Political posters on the walls look real, including the opposition's graffiti over them. There is a man carrying a gutted steer to the butcher to be rendered and packaged for sale. The steer is so freshly killed that its blood drips down the back of the man's white shirt.

During the explosion at the oil rig, Friedkin gives us a perfectly composed shot that could have been from a horror film. While showing the intense sheets of fire, the camera pans down to show a burned and dismembered arm laying on the ground, fingers outstretched as if trying to catch a ball. We only see this for a second, and it didn't even register the first time I saw it. I thought it was a burning wooden beam. It is such a powerful image I could see it being used as an alternative movie poster.

After multiple viewings, I noticed a neat bit of foreshadowing involving Roy Scheider's character. During the introductory vignettes of each character's past, we see his involvement with an Irish gang in New York robbing a church controlled by the mafia. After the heist, Scheider drives the escape car but wrecks it, resulting in the deaths of the three other gang members. The car smashes into a fire hydrant, which then spews water high into the air. Scheider emerges from the car bloody and dazed. He is drenched by the water. An hour further into the film, his character will again be drenched by the torrential rains as the trucks are crossing a rope bridge over the river.

Tangerine Dream, the German electronic band, were chosen to compose the soundtrack. This was their first American soundtrack, and it led to many others during the '80s including *Thief, The Keep, Flashpoint, Firestarter, Legend* and *Near Dark*. Their music is married to the visuals and was an excellent choice on Friedkin's part. Tangerine Dream's music is perfectly used in the scene where the men are working laboriously to repair the dilapidated trucks into workable shape. The moving camera, close-ups on rusted shock absorbers and bolts, and shots of everyone's sweaty bearded faces is a great montage sequence. As the trucks are finally refurbished to a drivable state, the music accentuates the action as they are, in essence, reborn. There is a shot of the main truck in silhouette, backlit in the rain. As the men turn on each of the work lights on the cab, there is a different musical cue for each light. The music is very pulsating and had to be an influence on John Carpenter who creates very

A WILLIAM FRIEDKIN FILM

SORCERER

MUSIC FROM THE ORIGINAL MOTION PICTURE SOUNDTRACK BY

TANGERINE DREAM

similar soundtrack music. Friedkin loved the Tangerine Dream music so much that he set up speakers on set and would play bits of the soundtrack before each take to get everyone in the proper mood.

Speaking more about the two trucks, Friedkin went to great lengths to use sound and visuals to make them seem like living animals. Named Sorcerer and Lazaro, the trucks end up seeming like they are alive. Friedkin uses zoomorphism to do this in numerous ways. The most genius effort was adding actual sounds of a tiger and cougar growling when their engines rev. When I used to watch this movie on VHS tape at home, I never could hear this effect. But seeing it in theaters and on remastered BluRay, the growls are definitely layered into the audio mix, making the trucks seem dangerous and primal. Even the structural design of the trucks creates a sense of faces without being obvious or cartoonish. The white grill on the front of the truck reminds me of teeth. The placement of the headlights and vent holes reminds me of eyes. There are unusual venting slots on the hood that made me think of dinosaur ridges or the gills of a shark. The extended exhaust pipes on the sides of the cab look like horns, and when the exhaust fumes spew out it seems like the exhaled breath of a bull before charging.

There is a particular scene I want to highlight and, no, it isn't the infamous rope bridge scene. I feel that scene has been deservedly discussed at length and I have nothing new to add. I'll admit, at least, that it's the highlight of the movie and the sequence most people remember from it. The scene I want to examine occurs much earlier in the film. When the explosion happens at the oil rig, several local workers die and their burned bodies are returned to the townspeople. We witness the grief and rage of the locals, who know they're being exploited by this huge corporation. The company treats loss of life like collateral damage, an 'acceptable loss', and this impersonal attitude generates anger which builds and builds until the crowd begins to riot.

Now, most Hollywood films that try to stage a riot scene fail, I feel. There tends to be too many shots of extras who

don't really look angry enough, pumping their fists and chanting. But in *Sorcerer*, Friedkin coached the extras very well and I didn't have to suspend my disbelief to buy that they were actual villagers and not paid extras. The riot scene feels real, as if the director had stumbled across an actual riot and filmed it. Whip-pans, hand-held cameras and intentionally blurry shots all add to the realism. At first the crowd quietly and carefully lower the bodies of their comrades down from the truck. The burned and bloody corpses are wrapped in plastic, which makes them seem like a spider's cocooned prey. After the bodies are removed from the trucks, the crowd becomes enraged, wrenching rifles away from the soldiers and lighting both trucks on fire. Gunshots punctuate the air, and more soldiers arrive on horseback. It's pandemonium. The candlelit vigil immediately following this feels all the more solemn and reverential after the chaos of the on-screen riot. The townspeople carry the coffins through the street as the main characters sit listening to their sobbing; pondering the costs and the all-pervasive death.

Another scene I love is when Scheider's character breaks down and loses it in the jungle. He has come across an insurmountable blockade to their progress, as a huge tree has fallen across the mud road. This tree is taller and wider than their trucks and it seems their journey is at an early end. Scheider wades into the swamp on the side with a machete and starts hacking away at the small trees, in the mad hope of somehow carving an alternate path around the felled tree. He is in a frenzy, chopping wildly at these smaller trees despite knowing he will not achieve his goal no matter how many of them he attacks. This could be interpreted as a visual representation of how Friedkin felt, lost and overwhelmed as the budget skyrocketed and the weather resulted in failure and forced relocation for reshoots. That's Friedkin screaming waist-deep in the swamp waters, much like Herzog making *Aguirre, the Wrath of God*, and Coppola making *Apocalypse Now*.

Near the end, one of the surviving characters has a powerful moment where he breaks the fourth wall by looking directly at the camera. The camera slowly zooms in on his face, still bloody and bruised. This is an existential moment of realization, and his weary expression reflects the stress of this endeavor, the numerous costs paid.

He is resigned to his perceived fate. He then decides to ask the barmaid to dance, and it's a beautifully magical moment.

In his memoir 'The Friedkin Connection', the director says that the entire point of the film is summarized by the following dialogue exchange:

Manzon: Then he was just a soldier.
Blanche: No one is "just" anything.

Interpret this as you will, but definitely watch *Sorcerer* again with new eyes. No-one is *just* the persona they present in public. No-one is all bad or all good. No-one is *just* their job or their rank or their past. People change over their lives, and certain films change as we watch them at different points in our own lives. *Sorcerer* resonates more and more the older I get. And I love it for that.

# THE GRISSOM GANG

**by David Flack**

I've always found Robert Aldrich an interesting director. His CV covers pretty much all genres. I have a particular soft spot for four of his less well-known films - *Ten Seconds to Hell* (1959), *The Last Sunset* (1961), *Hustle* (1975) and *The Grissom Gang* (1971), the latter of which I'll be covering here.

*The Grissom Gang* is based on a controversial 1939 novel by James Hadley Chase. It was turned into an equally controversial film called *No Orchids for Miss Blandish* in 1948 (retaining the title of the original book), and attracted heavy criticism for its violence and sexual overtones which were deemed objectionable at the time. However, the '70s remake was not nearly as shocking to enlightened audiences. It came four years after the classic *Bonnie and Clyde*, and one can see how it borrows some of that film's atmosphere and style, as well as being reminiscent of Roger Corman's *Bloody Mama* (1970).

The plot concerns Barbara Blandish (Kim Darby), a heiress who is kidnapped by a gang of hoods. When they are wiped out by another, more organised gang, Miss Blandish finds herself taken prisoner and held to ransom by them. Complications arise when a mentally disturbed, psychotic member of the gang, Slim Grissom (Scott Wilson), falls in love with her.

The film makes its style clear right from the opening sequence, starting in a cheesy and humorous tone before suddenly throwing jarring viciousness into the mix. It is punctuated with violence throughout, and it is used very effectively.

The Grissoms are an uneasy, volatile group. They resemble a family unit but certainly aren't very cooperative or compatible. No-one in their right mind would describe them as a 'happy family'. They are led by Ma Grissom (Irene Dailey), who looks like a typical granny but is actually as tough as old boots and quite ruthless. Pa Doc Grissom (Don Keefer) is the opposite - he craves a quiet life and is clearly afraid of his wife. Slim seems slow-witted and is at times the butt of the gang's jokes, but they are all wary of him because they know he has psychotic tendencies and will just as soon kill someone as look at them. Similarly dangerous is Eddie Hagan (Tony Musante), the big-shot gang member who secretly thinks he should be in charge. He's happy to kill anyone he feels might betray the group. There are two other members too, mainly just henchmen, named Mace (Ralph Waite) and Wappy (Joey Faye).

Ma plans to get the $1,000,000 ransom money, then kill the girl rather than handing her back safely. She intends to keep the money for a while, investing it in a nightclub business (speakeasies were a good moneymaker in early 1930s America). One of the reasons Eddie is with them is that he is dating Anna Borg (Connie Stevens), a girl who hopes to achieve fame in showbiz. The ransom is duly paid, but Ma's plan is thrown into turmoil when Slim gets wind of what they're going to do to their hostage. He shocks

them by holding a knife to his mother's throat, swearing he will kill her instead of allowing Miss Blandish to die. This is a great scene, with Wilson showing his skill as an actor and his ability to be very convincing. Needless to say, the gang are surprised by his actions and realise their plan is in total disarray. From here, the story unravels in an always interesting and engrossing way. It offers little that hasn't been done before but is handled in an enthralling manner, becoming darker, bleaker and rather more depressing (for one character in particular) as it progresses.

It's fair to say the heiress Barbara Blandish does not have an easy time of it. She is alternately roughed-up, slapped, punched, sexually molested and shot at. Her exposure to this world of vice and violence is treated with stark matter-of-factness. Barbara, suddenly ripped away from her rich lifestyle, finds herself isolated with a dangerous criminal group who are living hand-to-mouth. Worse still, she finds herself the object of desire of a halfwit criminal, a man who repulses her. At one point, she verbally abuses Slim, reducing him to a blubbering wreck. When he tells Ma, she gives the hapless heiress a hell of a beating for upsetting her son.

Slim is persistent in his advances. He spends more and more time with Miss Blandish and promises he will not let anything bad happen to her. It doesn't escape the attention of the others how often he is with her, and they also notice the way he takes her gifts and dresses smartly in her presence. Inevitably, Slim wants to make the relationship sexual and these scenes are deliberately awkward. He comes across like a fumbling teenager with little-to-no sexual experience, and Barbara either resists him or does nothing at all which makes him increasingly frustrated. Barbara is sometimes fawned over by other members of the gang when Slim is not around, but nothing ever happens because they're too afraid of Slim's retribution. There is a rather good scene where Barbara confronts Slim about why she is still being kept as she feels sure her father must have paid the ransom by now. Slim explodes in frustration, and reveals that, yes, the ransom has been paid and the others have been planning to kill her. It's only thanks to him that she is still alive. At this point, Miss Blandish realises her only hope is to put aside her loathing of him and act like his lover. As a kind of 'reward', she lets him have his way with her. Her actions are like a survival mechanism, and Slim even says to her: "You don't have to love me. Just like me, and be nice to me." This is where *The Grissom Gang* differs from the 1948 film. In the earlier version, Miss Blandish does in fact fall in love with Slim, but in the 1971 film she never really does. She acts the way she does mainly for her own survival (and you can't blame her for that), though she does soften towards him near the end. She realises Slim genuinely loves her, but it is generally a one-way relationship (though the closing scene suggests she cares enough to be upset by

his eventual fate).

There's a subplot running throughout wherein Barbara's father (Wesley Addy) hires a private detective named Fenner (Robert Lansing) to find his daughter. Fenner follows a lead in the nightclub angle, and gains information from Eddie Hagan's moll which helps him close in on Barbara's whereabouts. When he learns Miss Blandish and Slim may be having an affair, he passes this news on to her father. Mr. Blandish is reviled, and delivers the powerful line: "Then to me, she would be better off dead".

During the final act, the tension that has been building throughout is released in a bloody, violent way. Most of the characters end up dead; those who remain alive are mostly devastated and realise they've lost something and are isolated and truly alone.

The film presents a cynical, far-from-rosy portrayal of human behaviour. This view of people is fairly typical of director Aldrich - he held a bleak view of the human species which he displays in most of his films. The heiress does what she must to stay alive, but ultimately finds herself more isolated than when she was first abducted. Her father is totally repulsed by her, and we doubt he feels any lingering love toward her at the end. Ironically, Slim is the only character who stays true to any kind of values, as warped and twisted as they may be.

When first released, the film was not well received. As the years have gone by, it has received more favourable notices. It is not hailed as one of Aldrich's best, but I consider it underrated and find it somewhat enthralling. There are a number of good performances, especially Wilson as Slim. That's no surprise - he's one of my favourite actors and

a very unheralded talent. His performances always stand out - in my article about *The Ninth Configuration* (1980) in 'Cinema Of The '80s' Issue #1, I offer further praise for his work. In *The Grissom Gang*, he runs a variety of emotions - awkwardness, insecurity, vulnerability - while conveying cold-bloodedness and psychotic behaviour very believably. He got the role on the strength of his impressive performance in *In Cold Blood* (1967), beating Bruce Dern to the part of Slim. Mind you, Dern would have been good too, if a bit typecast. Darby is not the first actress to come to mind for the part of Barbara Blandish (Barbara Hershey was considered and may have been better). Apparently Darby didn't enjoy the role and described the film as "awful", perhaps because she was accustomed to playing more clean-cut characters in more clean-cut movies. Her revulsion comes across in her performanc and, if anything, makes the way she plays it more effective. She conveys despair, isolation and desperation almost from the start, doing what she must to survive while never being dealt a good hand. She will always be best known for her role in *True Grit* (1968). In *The Grissom Gang*, she is perpetually on edge. The scenes between her and Wilson are uncomfortable to watch, and they work because the two performers do their job so well.

Darby's best scene is her reaction to a violent incident that happens in front of her. She looks repulsed and terrified, and any hope goes right out of her with a piercing scream. You cannot help but feel pity for her. By the end, you know instinctively there is no rosy future in store.

I should also mention Musante as Eddie Hagan. He is very good as someone who is as much a psychopath as Slim, cold-bloodedly murdering anyone he feels may betray him or his ambitions. An inevitable clash between the two happens over Barbara, and the only surprise is that it hasn't happened sooner. The two other female members of the cast also register well. Irene Dailey is very good as Ma, showing a vicious streak and a mean mind while remaining fearful of her son's anger and instability (though she undoubtedly loves him). Connie Stevens provides some glamour as a classic gangster's moll. Her ambition to become a showbiz star, and her naivety and jealousy, mark her out as doomed. There is more than a hint of Marilyn Monroe in her looks and performance.

Overall, *The Grissom Gang* is a good entry in the gangster genre. Although clichés are present, it moves at a good lick and is always fascinating and entertaining. If you like the genre, the chances are you'll enjoy this.

# DARK PLACES

## Dark in places, yet cosily familiar

by Ian Taylor

*Beware, all ye who enter here, for yonder lie spoilers...*

Come and hold my hand, I'm going to take you to *Dark Places*. No, not the 2015 film based on the novel by Gillian Flynn. We're going further back than that, decades in fact... back to the early '70s, when the UK filmmaking industry wasn't quite on its arse and it was possible for distinguished actors to make low-budget horror films with a generally straight face. A time when those in front of and behind the camera produced films which looked richer than their budgets ought to have allowed. We are looking at the independent film *Dark Places*, made in 1972, though not released until the following year (or 1974 in some territories). This movie rested on my to-watch list for many years before I viewed it, and now that it has again resurfaced on Severin's Eurocrypt of Christopher Lee Volume 2 Blu-ray boxset (an uncut 4K scanned version taken from an internegative recently discovered in a London lab vault), it seems the ideal time to share my thoughts.

So, off we go. Hold my hand tightly though. It might all seem terribly familiar, but there are always twists and turns and you never really know what might suddenly

appear from those Dark Places...

Compared with many British genre films of the time, this particular piece seems to provoke puzzlingly few fond memories. Contrary to the likes of, say, *The Creeping Flesh*, *Horror Express*, *Asylum* or *Dracula AD 1972*, audiences seem either completely ignorant of its existence or, worse still, mildly critical in their remarks about it. It's as if any stronger feelings seem wasted on a film as minor as *Dark Places*.

As I finally sat down to watch it, I couldn't help but wonder why it is, and has been, so disregarded. With a cast of Brit horror favourites of the era - including Christopher Lee, Herbert Lom, Joan Collins and hammy old Robert Hardy - I figured it must surely must have some good things going for it. As the opening credits pan across a large country house resting in the shadows of night-time, and that favourite old technique of pathetic fallacy adds the sound of cold wind and rustling trees beneath an insistently nudging score, I began to realise that maybe the familiarity of all its iconography was working against it. "Move along now, sir, nothing of interest to see here!"

A car rolls up to what turns out to be a private asylum,

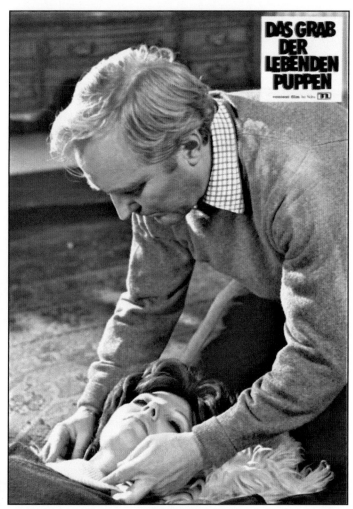

Wallace's, Mary Roberts Rinehart's and Ethel Lina White's canon of the 1920s. Such stories wound up as successful plays a few years later, then became staples of repertory theatre before being made into silent films and then remade in creaky sound a few years later, maybe into the '40s at the very latest. They were old by the time Vincent Price made *The Bat* in 1959, positively pointless by the time of Hammer/William Castle comedy-horror *The Old Dark House* (1963), and certainly well out of fashion by the '70s. Don't make the mistake of lumping it in with the likes of the excellent *The Legend of Hell House* (1973), either. That was all about faith (in religion, science or whatever), sexual repression and the investigation of a haunted house. In other words, completely different to traditional old dark house fare, which tends to be about hidden wealth, grasping affiliates and secret passages. Of course, there were exceptions - remakes of old dark house classics such as *The Cat and the Canary*, *The Spiral Staircase* and *Seven Keys to Baldpate* and the flawed but interesting Frankie Howerd vehicle *The House in Nightmare Park*. But all those films divide opinion and none can be described as a runaway success. Make no mistake about it, when it arrived on cinema screens *Dark Places* was a film out of time. Yet the more I watched, the more I began to realise I really was enjoying myself immensely and I wondered why.

and the window rolls down to reveal a terse Lee, just the right side of bombastic, on his way to visit a typically overcooked Hardy who appears to be in charge of the institution and is accepting the bequeathing of a stately home from Old Marr who is breathing his last. As well as the asylum and an old dark family pile, there's a hidden inheritance and scheming acquaintances, all hoping to get their grubby little mitts on the property and the money. It's all very old-fashioned in presentation, right down to regular horror bit-part player Roy Evans (*The House That Dripped Blood*, *Dr. Jekyll & Sister Hyde*, *Vault of Horror*) as the taxi driver who does a double take when Hardy's character, Edward Foster, tells him he's the new owner of Marr's Grove. "It's bad," he mumbles. "Things *happen* there…"

Yet surely we love all this stuff, don't we? Those lovely shots of a '70s railway station and a quiet English country village populated sparsely with cars from another age? We Brits love the nostalgia they evoke as much as the horror tropes. And our American cousins generally love getting glimpses of a green and pleasant land that, to be honest, most Brits probably don't see half as often as people think (if ever).

I think the issue here might be that the film is distinctly old-fashioned even for its time. It's basically an old dark house story, the sort of thing that was prevalent in Edgar

Surely some of the praise deserves to land fairly and squarely at the director's door. Don Sharp already had quite a pedigree by the early '70s. He was responsible for monochrome winners like *Witchcraft* and *Curse of the Fly*, and had previously worked with Christopher Lee on a lively selection of historicals including Hammer's *The Devil-Ship Pirates* and *Rasputin: the Mad Monk* and the first two Lee-starring *Fu Manchu* films. It was his first foray into horror that really commanded attention. The wonderful *The Kiss of the Vampire*, which he made in 1962 for Hammer, was a nicely atmospheric piece that successfully coped without Cushing or Lee and created a whole separate mythology for the titular monsters. Most interestingly, despite the

expected Hammerisms (e.g. the lovely atmosphere and the up-to-date colour and classiness the company brought to the genre), *Kiss* is actually quite old-fashioned. If nothing else, it showed us that Sharp was comfortable being let loose on outdated and hackneyed themes. Ten years later he would be at it again with *Dark Places*.

Sharp manages to create a sense of doom and dread without getting too carried away. His one misstep is in the scene featuring a hopelessly contrived country walk as Edward Foster (Hardy) begins to succumb to the grip

of the house and its past occupants. The use of reverb on the voices might have been enough, but the slow-motion camera work tips it over the edge and the fisheye lens effect positively kills the scene. Add to that an overplayed moment of possessed sleepwalking and talking from Hardy and the result is overdone and heavy-handed. Other than that, the director proves his abilities by presenting many spooky if cliched scenes in a subtle and unfussy way, letting the tale spin itself, steadily drawing the viewer in. He also knows how to use the performers to their best. Herbert Lom comes across as an almost cuddly and avuncular notary - but can he be trusted? As Prescott, the lawyer overseeing the legal affairs pertaining to the house, he is

well at home as a red herring, never pushing the enigmatic looks too far and remaining truthful in performance, even when cowering from a pick-axe attack near the end.

Lee, playing the deceased Marr's doctor, could do this sort of thing in his sleep but there's considerable gravitas in his performance when he reveals that Old Marr not only murdered his wife and lover in the house but also his children. And despite being revealed as a chiseller in search of Marr's hidden cache of cash early on, he never resorts to telegraphed twitches and gestures. He responds with palpable distaste when his sister Sarah (Collins) resorts to bedding Foster as a means of finding the money. Joan

herself, whilst offering to be the least likely housekeeper ever, is at home in her standard ice-maiden/scheming bitch/ horny slut role. In fact, she was ploughing the same furrow in *Fear in the Night* that very same year alongisde Peter Cushing Here, though, a warm façade masks her intent, and Sharp coaxes from her a performance that makes it believable that Foster might unsuspectingly fall into her honey trap. Even Hardy is kept calm for prolonged spells, though his shouty blustering inevitably wins out.

It's not just the actors that Sharp handles well. His shots of Foster arriving at the dilapidated entrance to Marr's Grove are well done, complete with an overgrown driveway and a 'Keep Out' sign juxtaposed effectively with the happy sounds of chirping birdsong. The unlocking of the allegedly haunted house allows for great scenes of dusty, dishevelled emptiness as Foster wanders from room to room, prompting the audience to shout: "No way would I be doing that!"

To truly appreciate how well Sharp does with his directing, and to understand why *Dark Places* is effective, we should really take a run though a checklist of old dark house iconography, a busy semantic field of old-fashioned horror imagery.

In some ways it could all be considered a bit silly... Foster's first action after being warned away by the taxi driver is to immediately put his leg through rotten floorboards. Step away everyone! Hardy in the hole! But other moments, whilst overly familiar, hit the right notes: a sinister doll with a broken face, a mysterious young woman waving from an upstairs window, a knife falling from who knows where and embedding itself into the floorboards, glass picture frames cracking across the image contained within, a moving rocking horse. These should get you thinking along the right lines, and it's so far so "Brr!" They all work pretty well, despite some overly booming music (courtesy of Wilfred Josephs who also provided the soundtrack to other '70s horrors such as *Cry of the Banshee* and *The Uncanny*) and Hardy's unnecessarily beefy roaring and shouting when the lights won't come on, leaving him to search in the dark.

There are other moments which work much better in their quiet simplicity. Whilst staying with Prescott the lawyer, Foster looks out of his bedroom window towards the silhouette of his stately pile on the horizon and, just visible through the dark night, notices a light on upstairs! On happening again later, Foster is informed that the window in question is the nursery of the murdered children. The notion is chilling, more so through its underplaying - let's face it, ghostly or evil children are always good for a shiver (ask anyone from Mario Bava and John Wyndham to the directors of *The Exorcist* and *The Omen*!) And so, when continuing a cash quest through the old house, Foster finds broken dollies everywhere and hears the giggling echoes of youngsters past.

Then there are other recognisable images and themes: a search for secret panels as a lurker lurks nearby, doors silently swinging open, dust sheets shifting unaided. The typical old dark house shenanigans are gradually overtaken by supernatural ones, and it was around this point that I realised the reason I was enjoying the hackneyed old clichés was because they were like old friends. I enjoyed the comfortable discomfort of a greatest hits of nostalgic terrors. A framed portrait of Old Marr in better years reveals an unlikely similarity in appearance to Foster. The next time he sees it, the image on the picture displays a slashed throat! Over here, there are mouldy footprints stepping across his bedroom; over there, he finds a pickaxe and uses it to reveal a secret room behind the fireplace that remains stubbornly out of bounds. The use of the tool to open up a hole results in one of the film's finest scenes of underplayed terror as Sharp keeps a firm directorial grip on a sudden rush of awakened bats from within the darkness beyond.

Perhaps even more impressive is how the director presents flashbacks to the time when Marr and family lived in the house, cleverly conveying Foster's descent into madness and a possible possession by the ghosts of the past. It's handled by having Foster step off camera from one scene and directly into another where he becomes

Andrew Marr (no, not the Scottish political journalist of BBC television fame), dressed in a dinner suit and sporting a handsome moustache. Just as we recover from that surprise, we realise the dilapidated house is now returned to its former glory. The wreck of the nursery complete with broken dolls is now clean and tidy, warmly decorated and full of unbroken toys. These scenes begin to escalate, eventually bringing in troubled wife Jean Marsh (a lovely portrayal of fragile sanity and desperate attempts to hold the family together while keeping madness at bay - the following decade, she would be appearing Stateside in a real haunted house classic, The Changeling) and the housekeeper/mistress Jane Birkin (remember the spooky scene of a woman waving from the upstairs window?) For now, though, the kids remain heard but not seen (I'm sure that traditionally we prefer it the other way around), their unnerving whispers and giggles reverberating around the old house, but they will eventually appear as the tale reaches its climax. Even unseen, they are a very tangible presence, whether as ghosts or lurking just out of sight during the regression scenes which continue to cleverly link past with present. In fact, these children strike me as being almost a reverse of the brother and sister in Jack Clayton's classic The Innocents. In that case, the children were influenced by the suggestion of ghosts, whereas here they are the ghosts. Both are clearly influenced by the unpalatable behaviour of the adults around them.

Sharp doesn't just smoothly segue from past to present and back either, he also manages to operate the rollercoaster of emotions effectively by switching from a spooky scene to a relaxed daytime scene and getting the tone just right in both. Following the first regression sequence, we are treated to lovely bucolic images during the morning after as Foster takes a morning stroll with Prescott. We need these semblances of normality to help us believe that Foster has the tenacity and presence of mind to continue operating within occasionally sinister scenes and surroundings. If it were all 'Creep City Central', who would believe he would stay?

But the flips from 'now' to 'then' become ever more frequent and the tale to be told becomes clearer. A beautiful canal-side scene featuring such delights as a chugging narrow boat, old stone bridge and canal lock offers a charming break in tension as Foster escorts Sarah Mandeville (Collins) out. But suddenly yet slickly, she transforms into Alta (Birkin) from the past and romantic music plays as she urges the younger Marr to have his wife and children committed to a mental institution so that he can make off with the housekeeper.

The children are finally seen in the next regression sequence, highlighting the escalation in the (possibly) supernatural occurrences and Foster's unbalanced state of mind. By this point, the story, familiar as it is, has become utterly engaging. I found myself on the edge of my seat as Foster sleepwalks his way to finding a hidden key within his fireplace, one which might unlock the hidden room and, perhaps, a hidden fortune. However, after yet more mental crumbling, Foster awakens on a doctor's couch to find both Lee and Lom towering over him - heh, heh, heh! Imagine how soothing that would make you feel!

At this point there is that tragic moment, so well done in British horror of the time as well as '80s anthologies like the *Hammer House of Horror* television series. That moment when the protagonist decides to give up and almost gets away before events transpire against them, or they change their mind - and then, all is lost!

I shall reveal no more as final stings in the tale occur (as we always expected they would) and people start to fall victim to the madness of one character or another. "I'm grown up too!" says Marr's little boy tellingly at one stage, followed by sinisterly cherubic smiles and "We can stay together always…" Perhaps they will, at that! Past and present merge effectively and, other than a gaping plot hole that shall remain un-named, everything is tied up effectively by the closing credits.

And there you have it. The old dark house tale given a '70s makeover, directed by a man who was Sharp by name and sharp in execution, and starring a veritable Who's Who of familiar names. And, as an added bonus, look out for a cameo appearance from John Levene as a doctor. Levene also appeared briefly in Sharp's wacky comic horror *Psychomania* (1972) but was best known for his regular role as Sergeant Benton of the UNIT military force in television's *Doctor Who* between 1968 and 1975. As an extra link to *Dark Places*, Levene appeared opposite the Third Doctor played by Jon Pertwee, who was once married to… Jean Marsh. Degrees of separation and all that!

*Dark Places* isn't top of the pile when it comes to '70s horror, but it deserves better than its relatively recent status as forgotten or disregarded. Much like another out-of-time old dark house film - *House of the Long Shadows* (1983) - it allows a selection of genre actors to have fun with a familiar scenario. If the viewer simply relaxes and immerses themselves as if in a warm bath of nostalgia, a good time ought to be guaranteed.

by Dawn Dabell

Peter Collinson's *Open Season* (1974) - based on a novel by David Osborn - depicts a man and a woman being held captive by a group of men who have a disturbing and perverse plan in store for them. As the story unfolds, we come to realise the poor captives are to be used as human prey by a group of hunters. Killing animals no longer satisfies their bloodlust. But hunting *people* for sport... now that really makes their juices flow!

Three friends and ex-Vietnam veterans - Ken (Peter Fonda), Greg (John Phillip-Law) and Art (Richard Lynch) - spend one week each year going on a hunting holiday minus their wives and kids. What they don't tell anyone is that the holiday isn't a chance for them to hunt game... instead, they kidnap people en route, enslave them, and eventually turn them loose and pursue them like wild animals. Their experiences in Vietnam have hardened them and made them hungrier for bloodsport of the extreme variety. Now it seems only a real manhunt can fulfil their violent and masochistic needs.

On the way to their cabin, they kidnap adulterous couple Nancy (Cornelia Sharpe) and Martin (Alberto de Mendoza) at gunpoint and force them along. Wrongly believing they have been kidnapped for a ransom, Nancy and Martin fail to grasp that they are really being set up to provide sport for the deranged war heroes. Upon arrival at the cabin, Nancy is chained up in the kitchen and made to carry out cooking and cleaning chores. Tensions between Nancy and Martin mount as it becomes apparent they are not looking out for each other but purely for themselves. As the days pass, the degradation inflicted upon the two captives increases. Martin finds himself taking on the cooking duties while Nancy is plied with alcohol and pawed over by Ken and Greg. When the odious trio have had their fun, they turn the couple loose. They give them a head start then attempt to track them and kill them.

Can Nancy and Martin elude their pursuers, or will they be hunted to their death?

Many compare *Open Season* to *Deliverance* (1972) in which some city men are terrorised by a group of hillbillies in the backwoods of Georgia. *Deliverance* is far more

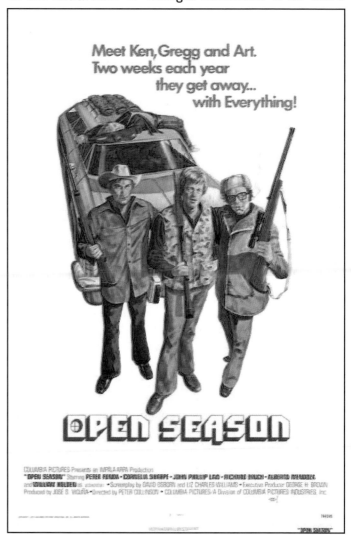

Meet Ken, Gregg and Art. Two weeks each year they get away... with Everything!

OPEN SEASON

COLUMBIA PICTURES Presents an IMPALA-ARPA Production "OPEN SEASON" Starring PETER FONDA · CORNELIA SHARPE · JOHN PHILLIP LAW · RICHARD LYNCH · ALBERTO MENDOZA and WILLIAM HOLDEN as associate · Screenplay by DAVID OSBORN and LIZ CHARLES-WILLIAMS · Executive Producer GEORGE H. BROWN · Produced by JOSE S. VICUÑA · Directed by PETER COLLINSON · COLUMBIA PICTURES-A Division of COLUMBIA PICTURES INDUSTRIES, Inc.

shocking and skilfully made, but I wouldn't necessarily place it in the 'hunting-man-for-sport' sub-genre. It's more about the city guys finding themselves in the wrong place at the wrong time, initially having to survive when they're attacked and sexually assaulted by the locals, then later having to deal with the consequences of fighting back with deadly force. For me, *Open Season* is a different kind of outdoor thriller, but it's a decent effort nonetheless.

*Open Season* also shares loose similarities with Sam Peckinpah's *Straw Dogs* (1971) which was extremely controversial when released due to its ambiguous rape scene(s). It has provoked debate ever since as to whether Susan George's character is raped by her ex-boyfriend or if she is a willing participant. Also, the second rape (in which George's character is undoubtedly not a willing participant) has long caused viewers to question what exactly is taking place - is she being sodomised or vaginally raped from behind? Whatever the answer, it is a very strong and uncomfortable scene to view. *Open Season* also features a rape scene early on - shown in in flashback - which implies that the victim has been raped vaginally <u>and</u> anally by her attackers. An attorney discussing the attack with the victim's mother mentions how she performed "acts of great perversion", which further hints at this.

Later in the film, Nancy has intercourse with one of her captors, Ken, but her willingness in the act is debatable. Nancy is drunk, afraid for her life, and has already flirted with Ken to try to find out what he and his buddies have in store for her and Martin. Can it be argued that she has figured out the danger and only has sex with him in order to save her own skin? There is also an uncomfortable thought - is she beginning to feel something towards Ken, in a 'Stockholm Syndrome' kind of way? This muddying of the waters (is she playing along to save herself, or does she believe she loves her captor and wants him to love her in return?) is reiterated several times as the film progresses. As with *Straw Dogs*, there's a whole debate to be had about whether it's rape or not and how much willingness or resistance was involved.

Some of the dialogue in the opening scenes emphasises why many rape victims feel they can't report their attacks. The attorney makes it extremely clear that no-one will believe this young female was 'had' against her will. The three males being accused are deemed upstanding members of the community, decorated war heroes no less, and alleging they did such horrific acts will fall on deaf ears. The attorney's comments are shocking, and his dismissiveness makes us feel anger and dismay. Yet more and more in the news, we hear reports of historical sex offences where the women or children involved explain how they tried to report being abused by someone in a position of power at the time but were ignored (especially if the accused was a well-regarded member of the community). It's an appalling response, but, as far-fetched as it seems when the attorney makes his awful remarks, we know from real-life that this can - and often does - happen. Later, there is another shocking throwaway remark by Martin, who says to the kidnappers: "why don't you just rape her and get it over with? She's drunk enough now." Hearing him say this about his girlfriend is pretty appalling. We expect him to try to put up at least some token resistance to protect her from such terrible acts, but instead he seems happy to let them to have their way with her as long as they don't hurt him.

Despite its exploitative themes, the film is tastefully handled. Most of the nudity is done in long-shot or obscured. Collinson could easily have taken the route of showing breasts, butts and pubic hair at every opportunity and it wouldn't have seemed out of place for a film from this era with this kind of plot. Even the scenes of violence, which escalate throughout, are handled with relative restraint. There's not a huge amount of blood and gore on show; most of the graphic stuff is shot from a distance. This generally helps the overall impact. The sustained suspense sequence at the end, in which guest star William Holden (as the father of the rape victim from the beginning) turns the tables of the trio of hunters, provides a satisfying wrap-up. Two endings exist, one where Holden drives his boat away at the end having achieved his gruesome revenge, another where he calmly turns himself in to the police after carrying out his vengeance quest.

*Open Season* is a well-made offering in the hunting-man-for-sport sub-genre. It really should be seen by fans of this type of thing, and will be of interest to fans of the director Peter Collinson, a tyrant behind the cameras by all accounts but responsible for a number of intriguing and fascinating films. It's not up there with the likes of *Deliverance* or *The Most Dangerous Game* but it's certainly worth 100 minutes of anybody's time.

# DEATH WISH

by Steven West

**"Until things change, stay away from New York City if you possibly can"** - 'Welcome to Fear City: A Survival Guide for Visitors to the City of New York' (1975 pamphlet)

While two standout horror films 25 years apart - *The Seventh Victim* (1943) and *Rosemary's Baby* (1968) - exposed Manhattanite Satanists, the decline of America's most populous city was also useful for exploitation cinema at the point where '50s nudie-cuties were superseded by Big Apple-based roughies like *Bad Girls Go to Hell* (1965). Here, you'd find misogynistic businessmen arming themselves with poisoned cat claws and bladed dildos, while wealthy New Yorkers crafted *Most Dangerous Game*-inspired urban safaris. Meanwhile, mainstream Hollywood awarded a Best Picture Oscar to an X-rated New York slice-of-life movie from a British filmmaker and a Polish cinematographer. 'Vanity Fair' defined *Midnight Cowboy*'s vision of N.Y.C. as a modern Sodom and Gomorrah. Alan J. Pakula's *Klute* further captured a rundown metropolis where the higher classes (plus their taxes) have escaped, poverty is rampant and Charles Cioffi's serial killer blames his rampage on the "sin, the glitter, the wickedness" of the city itself.

Bronx-born screenwriter Nicholas E. Baehr distilled the pressure cooker atmosphere of late '60s New York into *The Incident* (1967), in which disenfranchised Tony Musante

and Martin Sheen subject a subway car microcosm of the population to a night of terror. Crime rates were out of control and authority-defying counterculture movements spoke to a wider, growing distrust of law-enforcement. Cops were hamstrung by bureaucracy and the explosion of drug culture. New Hollywood movies like *Dirty Harry* (1971) gave audiences an outlet for frustrations on both sides: who wouldn't cheer when Callahan takes matters into his own hands, pursuing cinema's most loathsome serial killer before tossing his badge away as the credits roll?

While soaring violence in the '70s ultimately resulted in the formation of the vigilante gang the Guardian Angels (who gained support from Mayor Koch), Callahan ushered in a sub-cycle in which angry, victimised, mad-as-hell white men did what the rest of us didn't have the balls to do. New York novelist/historian Brian Garfield wrote dozens of books (often pseudonymous westerns) but was destined to be remembered for his 1972 'Death Wish' - cattily dismissed by Michael Winner as having sold three copies prior to the movie adaptation (two of them to Garfield's mother). In his memoir 'Winner Takes All',

43

the rambunctious filmmaker also shrugs off Garfield's 1975 sequel 'Death Sentence', conceived as a riposte to what he deemed the bastardizing of his novel en route to the screen. In 2007, when James Wan's remake emerged, New York counted 494 homicides in a population of over 19 million people, compared to 1691 among 8 million residents in the year 'Death Wish' hit the shelves.

At 160 pages, the novel is a model of economy, depicting the toxic existence of typical N.Y.C. residents: a collision of class/racial divides, smog, tourists, hookers, traffic jams and "concrete and plastic egg crate" housing. Before the story starts, overweight 47-year-old 'bleeding heart' liberal Paul Benjamin's wife has had her neck fatally twisted like a rag doll and his daughter has been brutally beaten into a state of catatonia. This horrific home invasion by three laughing young junkies is discreetly relayed in dialogue to a shell-shocked Benjamin - far from the graphic onscreen rape and humiliation in the first act of Winner's film.

Garfield assaults us with stats (200,000 addicts on the streets) and, amidst an escalating crime epidemic, gives us exhausted/jaded doctors and cops who are unable to offer reassurance that the perps will be caught. Benjamin's arc offers a potent portrait of a violent crime's aftermath: a little like spending time with the unseen, grieving parents of Scorpio's victims. Alienated, paranoid, swamped by endless sympathy cards and hyper-aware of potential threats on street corners, he rethinks his entire political stance, mentally reducing the city's inhabitants to "fodder"/"human cattle".

Benjamin's reference points are, like ours, Hollywood movies - he likens the muggers to stagecoach robbers in old westerns (while, like a typical '70s middle-aged man, deriding their long, scraggy hair) and watches choreographed violence and stylised car chases at the cinema between his armed nocturnal patrols. He's no hero: the violence he perpetrates is grimly described in terms of screaming agony, snapping heads, a dying boy shot in the face. His delusions of grandeur result in a self-portrait as a soldier of a new resistance, working for all those victims let down by the system. There is no comfort in knowing this unbalanced 'saviour' walks free at the end.

*Dirty Harry* and *Walking Tall* (1973) were thematically similar recent commercial smashes but, after financing the screenplay, United Artists dropped *Death Wish* - uneasy at the murderous protagonist and the challenge of casting the avenger (Jack Lemmon among the considerations). On the last day of filming another of the period's gritty rogue-cop thrillers, *The Stone Killer* (1973), Winner sparked Bronson's interest (based on the promise of getting to shoot muggers) in the script he'd acquired. This would be Winner's fourth (of six) pictures with the stoic, then-52 year old star - a union beginning with *Chato's Land* (1972) and which would now entirely pivot around his *Death Wish* protagonist. Perhaps reflective of charges of Fascism and racism aimed at Don Siegel's iconic hit, the Frank Yablans-headed Paramount, after committing to the picture, were still nervous about everything from the title (*The Sidewalk Vigilante* was considered) to depicting too many black muggers. Winner's answer was to cast a young Jeff Goldblum: "You don't have to worry about the blacks - I've just chosen the chief mugger, he's a Jew!"

As with every film from *The Games* (1969) onward, Winner acted as his own editor (under the pseudonym Arnold Crust) and, as with most after *The Jokers* (1966), his own producer. Though not entirely in 'Stone Face' mode, Bronson's casting inevitably shifts the novel into less complex urban western territory: the established western star's own taciturn Man with a Name preparing a lot more than four coffins. Garfield's challenging commentary on the modern culture of violence and the disturbing nature of vigilantism as a solution is largely abandoned. Paramount's trailer confirms how the cinematic *Death Wish* sought to appeal to 1974 cinemagoers: '70s Voiceover Trailer Guy brings a sarcastic joke ("Enjoy a typical afternoon in New York City…" as images from the home invasion unspool), while Bronson, here renamed Paul Kersey, is positioned as a what-we-need-right-now audience identification figure: "This is the story of a man who decided to clean up the most violent town in the world."

With the never knowingly subtle teaming of producer Dino De Laurentiis and Winner, and a script by Wendell Mayes (whose earlier credits include, appropriately, 1972's *The Revengers* in which rancher William Holden seeks those who killed his family and dog), it works hard to ensure we're too busy cheering on Bronson to question his actions. Kersey, a Korean War conscientious objector and architect (because no accountant ever looked like Bronson), is introduced in a calm-before-the-storm Hawaii beach prologue with his wife. Hope Lange, a then-recent Emmy-winner for *The Ghost & Mrs. Muir* (1968-70), sets a precedent for thankless female roles in *Death Wish* movies,

bringing fleeting humanity to the rare scene of intimacy: she poignantly frets about looking fat in holiday snaps. An effectively harsh cut hurls us into a typical outsider's view of 'war zone' New York City: freezing climate, rude locals, endless traffic, twenty-one murders a week.

Staging the catalytic assault changes everything. This joined a cycle of (in)famous early '70s British and American films showcasing oft-debated, oft-censored scenes of

sexual violence. In the era of *The Exorcist*, Goldblum's gang are given the harshest possible R-rated studio-film dialogue just so we know how evil they are: "I kill rich cunts." Winner wastes no time in stirring up the viewers' mob mentality: in still-distressing scenes, Lange is beaten and forced to watch her daughter's backside spray-painted before she is raped.

The immediate aftermath errs relatively close to Garfield via a city not conducive to victim support. Overwhelmed hospitals, ineffectual police, Kersey's dead wife and PTSD-suffering daughter are reduced to case numbers. Any given glance out of Kersey's window reveals another crime in progress. After withdrawing $20 of coins to load up a sock (just in case), he's almost immediately accosted by a knife-wielding would-be robber. In the most direct nod to *Death Wish*'s western roots, a work trip to a Tucson tourist attraction seals the transition from knee-jerk liberal dismissing the gun boys to realising Tucson by night is a safe place to walk and viewing a gun as "just a tool - like a hammer". As in the book, Kersey's first victim (an armed junkie) is left writhing in agony rather than perishing quickly like a shot western outlaw, and Kersey's response is to run home and vomit. Thereafter, however, he becomes a very Bronson-like efficient killing machine; subsequent shootings in alleyways and subways setting the tone for the sequels.

Winner isn't totally averse to Garfield's satirical streak: his Paul Benjamin memorably sits on the toilet reading press coverage of his cleansing efforts. The movie briefly depicts growing debate and media reports as Kersey's work becomes famous. Old ladies feel empowered to fend off muggers with hat pins and construction workers rough up bad guys while waiting for the cops. Dinner party discussions stoke the studio's fears of inciting racial hatred: guests question if The Vigilante is racist due to the colour of his main victims; one response, echoed by Winner himself, is "more blacks are muggers." Kersey becomes the cover star of all the big magazines, anticipating the fame and hero-worship that would await Travis Bickle in *Taxi Driver* two years later. The Mayor, anticipating the city's real-life political debates later in the decade, fears a vigilante wave and Kersey becoming a martyr but, with his city on the brink, encourages him to depart, while maintaining a public impression that he's still out there.

Ultimately, Winner plays it safe for the best commercial prospects and to avoid alienating the audience from Kersey's mission. The initial home invasion remains one of the most disturbing scenes of its decade; the equivalent in Eli Roth's disappointingly bland 2017 remake is notably mild by comparison, though John Schlesinger's underrated *An Eye for an Eye* (1996), includes a couple of the most unpleasant sequences in Hollywood vigilante cinema. After the difficult first kill, the 'punks' targeted by Kersey are all leery, one-note thugs perishing in ways no more visually violent than contemporary westerns. The jokey coda (one of Winner's own contributions) both reinforces Kersey as a hero-for-our-times while setting up potential sequels: arriving in a new city, he mimes a finger-gun action to a generic mugger after helping out a potential female victim.

The picture's huge success paved the way for everything from inventive, subversive indies (Abel Ferrara's 1980 *Ms.45*) to hardcore porn, with the splendid *Sex Wish* (1976) starring *Deep Throat*'s Harry Reems as a lawyer whose castration-laced roaring rampage of revenge (following his fiancée's graphically conveyed violation) is intermittently interrupted by lively threesomes. Though referring, in 1975, to his own film as a "one-joke" affair, Winner would embrace the vigilante theme again in his final two films. *Death Weekend* (1993) was sold as a female *Death Wish* - though its failure prompted Winner to suggest the notion (from Helen Zahavi's novel) of a young woman killing lowlife scum lacked the allure of Bronson or Eastwood doing the same. *Parting Shots* (1998) has Britain's own Charles Bronson, Chris Rea, playing a terminally ill character offing the people who most jarred him in life.

Often wheeled out for censorship debates in Video Nasties-era England, Winner passionately opposed censorship while emphasising the comic book overtones of his Bronson series, insisting there was always a "certain winking at the audience going on" and positioning the default 'mugger' villains as merely a modern equivalent to old-school antagonists like "the wicked king or the American Indian." Heavily cut in both the U.S. and the U.K., the Cannon-produced *Death Wish II* (1982) abandons the liberal dilemma of the source material in favour of unapologetic vigilante propaganda. Winner upped the ante with a fresh home invasion that errs far closer to the realm of *Last House on the Left* than you'd expect from a sequel to a Hollywood hit with a big-name star. He also brought back Vincent Gardenia's comic, cigar-chomping, flu-ridden detective from *Death Wish*, albeit mostly so he can dramatically perish while reciting the Lord's Prayer.

By the time of Winner and Bronson's final collaboration, the loveably daft *Death Wish 3* (1985), the punks looked like a parody of scaremongering 'Daily Mail' headlines, the western influence extended to a Winner-zoom into a cowboys-and-Indians painting and Bronson's new neighbourhood breaks out into spontaneous applause after Kersey guns down a gang leader - like a pro-vigilante version of the NHS clap.

*Death Wish 3* was released almost a year after mugging victim Bernhard Goetz shot four teenagers on a Manhattan subway train - sparking major debates in the U.S., a strong degree of hero worship (Goetz ran for Mayor in 2001), critique of the police and a call for direct action to tackle the crime rate. While Goetz was immortalised by Billy Joel's *We Didn't Start the Fire* and an inspiration for the anti-heroes of *Falling Down* (1993) and *Joker* (2019), Winner was characteristically amusing when asked for his views on the Kersey-like actions of the so-called 'Subway Vigilante', telling Melody Maker: "I don't approve of what Mr. Goetz did. But I have to say, that if he has to shoot anybody on the subway, I wish he'd do it on the week we're opening."

# Woody Allen's '70s
## A Decade of Creative Evolution

by Brian Gregory

During the '70s, Woody Allen was a prolific writer and director of successful comedy films that remain beloved to this day. These movies would become increasingly progressive and dynamic as the years went by, forming the basis of a sophisticated, existentialist style that he further developed in the following decades. Allen's hit-rate during this period is astounding, creating a number of hilarious movies that would go on to become all-time classics. His "early, funny" works include (in order of release): *Bananas* (1971), *Play It Again, Sam* (1972), *Everything You Always Wanted To Know About Sex\* (\*But Were Afraid to Ask)* (1972), *Sleeper* (1973), *Love and Death* (1975), *Annie Hall* (1977), *Interiors* (1978) and *Manhattan* (1979). He also starred in *The Front* (1976) but did not write or direct this film.

In this decade, Allen's comedy would evolve and shift from pure slapstick to a more mature and romantic style of comedic drama, and we'll witness this incredible progression as we examine his written and directorial output during those ten fruitful years.

## Bananas (1971)

In 1971, on the back of his successful play, *Play It Again, Sam*, Allen was offered a three-picture deal by United Artists. *Bananas*, the first of these, is loosely based on the book 'Don Quixote USA', a 1966 novel by Robert Powell. So loosely in fact, that when Arthur Krim, the head of United Artists, realised that it bore little resemblance to the novel he'd bought the rights to, he wanted to sue Woody for fraud. The film was largely shot in Puerto Rico and became a surprise hit for UA. This, despite having, as

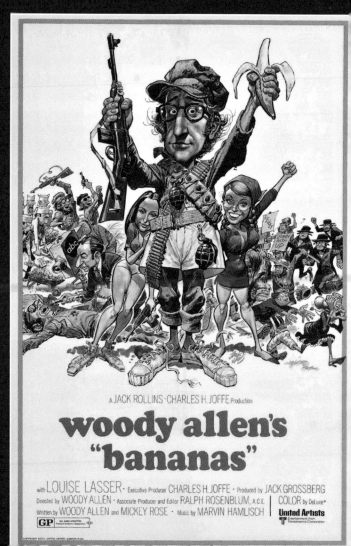

A JACK ROLLINS · CHARLES H. JOFFE Production

## woody allen's "bananas"

with LOUISE LASSER · Executive Producer CHARLES H. JOFFE · Produced by JACK GROSSBERG
Directed by WOODY ALLEN · Associate Producer and Editor RALPH ROSENBLUM, A.C.E.
Written by WOODY ALLEN and MICKEY ROSE · Music by MARVIN HAMLISCH

COLOR by DeLuxe®

United Artists
Entertainment from Transamerica Corporation

GP ALL AGES ADMITTED Parental Guidance Suggested

Woody later recalled, "No plot and lots of insanity."

The title of Allen's satirical slapstick film translates as 'crazy' and the plot certainly lives up to this meaning. It was written by Allen with Mickey Rose and is set in a fictional Banana Republic (San Marcos) where the president is killed in a coup d'etat plotted by a corrupt general. Meanwhile, in New York, a neurotic blue-collar worker, Fielding Mellish (Allen), meets attractive political activist Nancy (charmingly played by Louise Lasser, Woody's real-life wife from 1966-70) while she is out canvassing support for democracy in the aforementioned Latin country, and they fall in love. However, Nancy soon sees Fielding as an immature man with no leadership qualities and dumps him. In a desperate effort to impress her, Mellish decides to head to San Marcos and join the revolutionaries, where he helps win the revolution and eventually ends up as President.

The uniquely Woody Allen idea of covering a South American revolution as a sporting event works wonderfully and convincing the voice of American sports himself (Howard Cosell) to join in the fun gives an authenticity that adds much to the film's successful satire. In fact, it's quite startling how so much of this movie still has relevance today, with Cosell's announcer predating our current experience of news as entertainment. Among all the gags and absurdity, Allen manages to expose the CIA as the true enemy within, while also mocking both the Cold War and liberal left. The mass media, politicians and even casual viewers are also unwitting targets of Allen's satirical eye.

To accompany the mayhem on screen, future Bond composer Marvin Hamlisch provides a suitably absurd and complimentary score, featuring playful tunes to juxtapose the movie's dark commentary (which includes the assault of an elderly lady by a fresh-faced and uncredited Sylvester Stallone). The film's memorable conclusion, where Woody goes to great lengths to explain what a sham trial is, really hits the mark: "I object, your honour! This trial is a travesty. It's a travesty of a mockery of a sham of a mockery of a travesty of two mockeries of a sham."

His second self-directed film (after 1969's *Take the Money and Run*) *Bananas* is a reminder of the young Woody's instinctive comic gifts, albeit with few signs of the philosophical filmmaker that would later emerge. It works largely off his stand-up aesthetic, which mixed comedy with intellectual musings, and we are reminded not only of Allen's legendary one-liners, but also his smart sight gags and highly creative physical routines. Packed with a never-ending conveyor belt of jokes and a ton of zany energy (clearly inspired by his love of Charlie Chaplin and The Marx Brothers) *Bananas* still has much to admire and laugh at all these years on.

## Play It Again, Sam (1972)

Based on Allen's 1969 play of the same name, *Play It Again,*

*Sam* cleverly blends the comedic with the romantic. It reveals Woody taking a step towards his cinematic future, while still playing the prankster that American television had come to love him for. The film is also notable for the first appearance of Diane Keaton in his movies and for being directed by Herbert Ross, rather than Woody.

Allen plays film critic, Allan Felix, another neurotic, socially awkward and clumsy character. Felix's all-time favourite movie is *Casablanca*. It's an obsession of his which he uses as a means to avoid the occupational and romantic turmoil in his life. Meanwhile, the star of *Casablanca*, Humphrey Bogart (his hero), regularly turns up in ghostly fashion throughout the film to give Felix advice on romance and masculinity. While his closest friends, a married couple named Dick (Tony Roberts) and Linda (Keaton), constantly try to help him find love by introducing him to prospective partners. Mirroring the plot of *Casablanca*, these all end in complete disaster, only for Allan and Linda to realise that they have fallen in love with each other. Much soul-searching and hilarity ensues.

Among the film's many highlights, is the classic art gallery exchange between Woody and a beautiful girl - who is even more depressed than he is. This may well be the first clip I ever saw from a Woody Allen film. Despite being a film junkie, I discovered his movies quite late, but after chancing upon this scene I was a fan for life:

Interior. Museum.

Allan: That's quite a lovely Jackson Pollock, isn't it?

Museum Girl: Yes, it is.

Allan: What does it say to you?

Museum Girl: It restates the negativeness of the universe. The hideous lonely emptiness of existence. Nothingness. The predicament of Man forced to live in a barren, Godless eternity like a tiny flame flickering in an immense void with nothing but waste, horror and degradation, forming a useless bleak straitjacket in a black absurd cosmos.

Allan: What are you doing Saturday night?

Museum Girl: Committing suicide.

Allan: What about Friday night?

Only in a Woody Allen film would its best punchline be about committing suicide.

Woody gives one of his strongest performances here and his chemistry with the excellent Keaton is obvious throughout, although she isn't called upon to be a comedic foil in this role, more a sympathetic cheerleader for his neurosis. Elsewhere, Jerry Lacy provides a decent Bogart impersonation and the ever-underrated Tony Roberts (admirably playing his role dead straight) constantly updating his locations and phone numbers to his answering service remains a highlight.

Something not often mentioned regarding *Play It Again, Sam* is the excellent set design. Allan's New York apartment and stereo system set up in this film remain ironically very cool (possibly too cool for the character), as is (in one scene) his green beatnik cardigan, which Kurt Cobain may have been influenced by when he dressed almost identically for Nirvana's legendary MTV Unplugged Show, appropriately filmed in New York, 20 years later. Woody as fashion influence on the king of grunge rock? Well, they certainly shared a love of darkly cynical humour, so why not cardigans too?

While *Play It Again, Sam* can be said to lack the emotional depth of Allen's later films, it has an undeniably attractive charm that brilliantly blends fantasy with reality and compliments its romantic comedy conventions. It was also Allen's first onscreen appearance that did not revolve purely around slapstick (though this is still prevalent here), a clear precursor to *Annie Hall* and an important part of his filmic journey and development.

## Everything You Always Wanted to Know About Sex* (*But Were Afraid to Ask) (1972)

Woody's next film was *Everything You Always Wanted to Know About Sex* (*But Were Afraid to Ask)*, a sex comedy anthology film based on the book of the same name by David Reuben. Allen wrote and directed the screenplay, which is split up into seven different vignettes, each

depicting a story related to an erotic enquiry. Clearly influenced by the anarchic television comedy of *Monty Python's Flying Circus* with its sketch-style format and chaotic, deliberately offensive humour, Allen's DNA nevertheless remains all over these skits. Of course, as with all sketch films, it is a rather hit and miss affair (the transvestite sketch, in particular, has dated badly and does not play at all well now) but there are several comedic bullseyes within.

The seven vignettes are:

1. *Do Aphrodisiacs Work?* A court jester (Allen), who desires the Queen (Lynn Redgrave), obtains a love potion.

2. *What is Sodomy?* A doctor (Gene Wilder) falls in love with a sheep and embarks on an illegal affair which lands him in big trouble.

3. *Do Some Women Have Trouble Reaching Orgasm?* Gina (Louise Lasser) finds that horny husband Fabrizio (Allen) does not turn her on, but sex in public places does.

4. *Are Transvestites Homosexuals?* Sam is caught trying on

**5.** *What Are Sex Perverts?* Celebrities try to guess a guest's special preferences on a TV game show-*What's My Perversion?*

**6.** *Are the Findings of Doctors and Clinics Who Do Sexual Research and Experiments Accurate?* Victor Shakapopolis (Allen) meets up with an eccentric scientist, Dr Bernardo, whose latest experiment (a giant breast) breaks free.

**7.** *What Happens During Ejaculation?* Woody plays sperm #1 and becomes anxious about his fate.

Allen incorporates a variety of filming styles to answer his various questions - from European Arthouse to '50s B-movie. Much wacky fun is on offer, it's often laugh out loud funny and the cast are superb. There are many highlights: Gene Wilder's character in *What is Sodomy?* is named Dr. Doug Ross, which was later the name of George Clooney's character on *ER*. It's an amusing sketch with Wilder falling in love with a sheep. However, John Carradine possibly steals the film as the mad scientist who creates all manner of bizarre sexual experiments, including making a giant boob, which eventually breaks free from his laboratory and goes on a murderous killing spree! It's a funny homage to the work of Ed Wood and other schlocky horror movies of its period. In the final segment, comes the sperm. This iconic scene would go on to influence everything from *Herman's Head* to *Inside Out*.

Many viewers will enjoy the surreal ideas on offer here and the performances perfectly compliment the script, which is another Woody gag fest. Apparently, Allen came out immediately after the film's release and admitted that he had included every single joke that he had ever thought of concerning sex. Later remembering the film as "My first big commercial success but while it had some funny things in it, not my finest." Personally, I learnt nothing at all about sex but enjoyed many of the jokes.

## Sleeper (1973)

For his next film, Woody changed genres and took a nostalgic look at the future in his sci-fi comedy, *Sleeper*. He plays nerdy Miles Monroe, a health store worker who has been cryogenically frozen for 200 years. Miles is awakened

by anti-government radicals in a strange futuristic world to assist them in over-throwing an oppressive, fascist government force. He unwittingly becomes part of the underground movement and causes a revolution. On his journey, Miles meets up with a spoiled rich woman Luna (Diane Keaton) and influences her (unintentionally) into becoming a revolutionary activist. *Sleeper* reveals an obscure Orwellian future where personal freedoms are limited, but everyone appears happy due to a combination of orgasm-creating machines and a healthy diet of cigarettes and fudge cake. Jokes fly out of the screen at

the speed of light and the lines are as witty as ever.

Luna: What's it feel like to be dead for 200 years?

Miles: Like spending a weekend in Beverly Hills.

Woody and his pal, the prolific TV writer, Marshall Brickman, came up with the basic script and showed it to science fiction heavyweights, Isaac Asimov and Ben Bova (also an uncredited science advisor for the film). They loved it, even going as far as praising the technological aspects. In fact, *Sleeper* would go on to win a Hugo and Nebula Award for best science fiction film. To add to *Sleeper's* sci-fi credentials, Douglas Rain was brought in to voice the evil computer and parody his performance as HAL in Stanley Kubrick's *2001: A Space Odyssey* (a film that Allen adored - while Kubrick himself was a huge fan of Woody's films).

Filming took place in Los Angeles, Monterey, Colorado and at the Culver City Studios. While shooting in the Rocky Mountains, Allen obsessively (just as many of his on screen personas would surely have done) checked his body every night for ticks. One night he found one and was convinced that he would need his leg amputated! Hypochondria is never far away from Woody Allen, both on screen and off. The Denver location was used as it had a number of futuristic looking structures, the most famous of these being Sculptured House, now known as Sleeper House because of its use in the movie. For costume design, future hit-maker Joel Schumacher (who went on to direct *The Lost Boys* and *Falling Down*) joined the team.

Allen initially envisaged *Sleeper* as a completely silent film that would enable him to indulge his love of Harold Lloyd, Buster Keaton and Charlie Chaplin. He soon realised that this wouldn't work for an entire feature, so kept the silent comedy concept for the scenes where he played a robot, as well as several hilarious chases. Indeed, with its slapstick nature and lively New Orleans ragtime musical score (which Woody played on), much of this movie seems to crave the silence of early 20<sup>th</sup> century cinema.

*Sleeper* is one of Allen's more accessible films, perhaps because it frames the gags and slapstick within a clever plot. Woody would later recall, "When I got to *Sleeper*, I started to develop more and feel the need for more of a story." Despite being a comedy, as with all well-written science fiction, it successfully uses the genre to not only imagine our future, but also to comment on the times in which it was written.

## Love and Death (1975)

After *Sleeper's* frantic journey into the future, Woody's next film would reverse his comedic time machine and take viewers way back to 19<sup>th</sup> century Russia in order to satirise Russian literature (the film's title itself being a play on *War and Peace*), history and classical philosophy.

Woody plays Boris Grushenko, a "militant coward",

**WOODY DIANE**
**ALLEN KEATON**

The Comedy Sensation of the Year!

**"LOVE and DEATH"**

A JACK ROLLINS - CHARLES H. JOFFE PRODUCTION

Produced by CHARLES H. JOFFE   Written and Directed by WOODY ALLEN

United Artists

the time of war with Napoleon. He's in love with his cousin, Sonja (Diane Keaton), and, similar to how a classic Russian novel may do, explores the meaning of life, via years of adventure, while dealing with personal philosophical struggles. In this challenging climate, both decide to kill Napoleon... but of course fail miserably.

Throughout the film, Woody parodies some of his biggest influences. References to Bergman appear in the character of Death (*The Seventh Seal*) and in an exchange between Keaton and Jessica Harper as they parody a scene from *Persona*. Dostoevsky and Tolstoy are also frequently referenced, which can be a problem in getting all the jokes if one is not up to speed on classic Russian literature. There is an entire scene containing dialogue between Boris and his father, with each line alluding to (or being composed entirely of) Dostoevsky titles. That said, the mass appeal of Allen's fish out of water comedy means there's still something for everyone to enjoy and plenty of laughs to be had. As with his other early films, it's filled with slapstick and there are plenty of moments where surreal, Pythonesque comedy makes another welcome appearance. For example, there's a marvellous war scene where all the soldiers are lined up for battle when a popcorn vendor suddenly comes into the frame. Wonderfully absurd, but it works perfectly. Woody also uses his recurring masturbation motif. When the Countess praises Boris as the greatest lover she ever had, he replies, "I practice a lot when I'm alone."

Allen does a fine job directing and his performance, as a deliberately anachronistic character, is up there with his best. For whatever reason, Woody's acting is often overlooked by critics, so focused are they on his dialogue, but this is an over-sight. When Woody was feeling inspired, his acting and comic timing are as good as anyone in the comedy genre and he surely deserves more credit than he receives. The rest of the cast of *Love and Death* are on top form too. In particular, the ever reliable Keaton, who is simply sublime. Her instinctive double act with Allen is a joy to behold. Their timing and chemistry is something that all aspiring actors should witness; they complement each other beautifully.

Aesthetically, *Love and Death* is the most visually impressive of Woody's films thus far. Ghislain Cloquet's cinematography is beautiful. The man behind the camera (and lighting) of cinematic, picturesque classics, such as Roman Polanski's *Tess*, offers richer imagery and content to assist Woody's continuing evolution as a director. In particular, the wide angle battle scenes of the Russians fighting Napoleon's armies are epic (reminiscent of scenes in Sergei Bondarchuk's *War and Peace*) while more intimate close up shots are perfectly framed. For the battles, shot in occupied Budapest, Woody used hundreds of Red Army soldiers, of whom he observed, "All they wanted was relief from occupying and cartons of cigarettes." Unlike

the visuals, the soundtrack proved difficult to get right at first. Allen tried Stravinsky but this clashed with the humour on screen, so he switched to Prokofiev. Woody remained satisfied with this particular musical choice years later, "The moment we did (use Prokofiev), the film came alive." Allen would later remember this movie as, "My favourite film. Even *Annie Hall*, which gave me real success, isn't as dear to me."

*Love and Death* is a parody that revisits and satirises Russian classics along with Russia's 19th century history. It's an impressive parody, covering existential themes that may inspire viewers to discover relevant books and artists or themselves. This film represents the last step in Allen's formative period before gaining a full focus on his unique film-making style. A style which would really blossom in his next project.

## Annie Hall (1977)

*Annie Hall* is perhaps the definitive Woody Allen film. It's the film where he fully realised his own cinematic style, blending hilarious observational comedy with bittersweet autobiographical reflection. The jokes are transparently a

...over for the character's genuine concerns • to escape, succeed and state the truth about all the pretension that surrounds him. This is not just Woody Allen being funny, it's Woody Allen showing us the absurdities and tragedies of life.

Allen plays Alvy Singer, a middle-aged, divorced, neurotic, stand-up comic. Alvy is a hopeless romantic who looks back on and deconstructs the failure of his relationship with Annie Hall, an insecure nightclub singer.

Divorced twice, Singer never seems to be able to sustain a relationship and we see why via a series of humorous flashbacks. However, when he accompanies his friend (Tony Roberts) to a tennis game he meets the titular Annie Hall (Diane Keaton). Initially, they appear to have little in common but something between them clicks and they embark on a highly volatile two-year romance.

Annie, superbly played by Keaton, is beautiful but quirky, fashion conscious yet carefree...and a very poor driver.

She is a Midwestern girl while Alvy is a lifelong New York Jew who's been seeing a therapist for many years (Annie only needs to see one after she's been dating Alvy for a while). Whilst Alvy is an introverted misanthrope, Annie is an extrovert singer. Yet, as in all classic screen romances, opposites attract and these perfectly flawed characters remain maybe the finest Allen ever created.

The script of *Annie Hall* (written with Marshall Brickman) is a work of art in itself and perhaps the most impressive example of their screenwriting. There is a plethora of quotable lines that are much more than mere throwaway one-liners. Here, each line has a poignancy coupled with its humour. Each line serves as a part of a greater whole. Each conversation is not only entertaining to listen to, but thoroughly believable. Every word spoken seems authentic, an authenticity greatly aided by the wonderful performances on display from the talented performers.

To complement his script, Woody proves his directorial development and growing self-confidence by using several cinematic techniques to reveal how the characters' relationship started, how it developed and where it ended up. These include inner monologue subtitles, the use of flashbacks, fast forwards, the breaking of the fourth wall and split screen. Cinematographer Gordon Willis also deserves praise as he uses his camera to cleverly invite the viewer into Alvy and Annie's world.

There are so many highlights in this film that it would be impossible to list them all, but as means of an example (or three) of its genius, some of my personal favourites would be:

When we see Annie and Alvy sharing

their rate of intercourse with their analysts, via the use of split screen. Alvy declares, "It's hardly ever, maybe three times a week." Simultaneously, in the other consultant's room, Annie has a very different opinion, "Constantly! I'd say three times a week!"

Memorably, a young Christopher Walken has a whole scene to himself. Playing Annie's younger brother Duane, he reveals to Alvy that when he is driving his car he has an urge to crash it and explode into flames. This is a brilliant set up for the next scene where Duane drives Annie and Singer to the airport and (as the camera pans from Walken to Allen) we see the fear written all over Alvy's face.

My top pick would likely be the sequence in the cinema line. Annie and Alvy are arguing as a pseudo-intellectual lecturer pontificates behind them in an effort to impress his date. Alvy just can't bear any more of him and (after breaking the fourth wall to share his frustration), with the pompous fellow queue member refusing to back down on his insights into Marshall McLuhan's work, Singer produces Marshall himself from behind a lobby placard. McLuhan bluntly informs the guy, "You know nothing about my work, how you got to teach a course in anything is totally amazing!" It's a fantasy that many a cineaste will have shared and Woody acknowledges the gratification in the viewer by having Alvy break the fourth wall once again, with the scene's concluding line, "Boy, if life were only like this!"

*Annie Hall* proved to be extremely popular with audiences and ended up winning four Oscars. Not that Woody was particularly enamoured by the success. On Oscar night he chose instead to play jazz with his band in New York, later commenting in typically cynical fashion, "It was fine I got an Oscar for directing, but what did that mean? Was my work improving? Was I taking enough risks? Did it stave off my crown baldness?"

For me, it's one of the finest films anybody has ever made and displays Allen's creativity, humour and scriptwriting at its absolute zenith. A peak that very few, if any, comedy writer/directors have reached before or since.

## Interiors (1978)

For his next film, Woody took on the challenge of writing a serious and introspective psychological drama. *Interiors* would be his first fully dramatic piece, a piece completely devoid of his trademark humour.

He'd always wanted his body of work to contain some high drama to sit alongside his more familiar comedic repertoire. This was an itch that he'd long needed to scratch. Deep down, Woody longed to be recognised as a serious writer and filmmaker - just like his cinematic hero, Ingmar Bergman. As a teenager, he had been impressed by the intellectual nature present in Bergman's films - such as *The Naked Night.* Of course, there are references to the Swedish legend's movies in much of Woody's work (as

we've seen, *Love and Death* is full of them) but for *Interiors* Woody wanted to remove such references previously used primarily for quick gags, looking this time for a similar pace and tone of filmmaking to that of his idol.

Specifically, Allen was inspired by *Persona* (1966) and *Cries and Whispers* (1972). As well as their poetic form, these two films starred women and were driven by female relationships. "Somewhere along the line - I don't know why or what happened - for some reason, I started to write basically from the woman's point of view all the time." Another key inspiration was Eugene O'Neill (most famous for 'Long Day's Journey into Night'). Setting aside the obvious inspiration, Woody felt that *Interiors* had more vitality and was less cold, less full of Swedish guilt than Bergman's work, seeing it as a film that was more akin to O'Neill's filmography.

In this movie, we meet three sisters, Flyn, Joey and Renata, all riddled with jealousies and insecurities, who are the daughters of separated, wealthy parents. Their father is a lawyer (played by EG Marshall) and their mother a mentally troubled (but perfectionist) interior designer, named Eve (a superb Geraldine Page). She is determined to make it on her own while retaining control over Joey, but has a mental breakdown and attempts suicide. When Marshall begins a new relationship with a down to earth lady named Pearl (Maureen Stapleton), who prioritises feelings over intellectual examination, this brings more pressure on the sisters, each of whom are individually dealing with their own psychological and emotional problems. Renata (Diane Keaton) is the eldest sister and a successful poetic writer but her husband feels overshadowed by her success and she has become disillusioned with her work. Flynn (Krystin Griffith) is an attractive television actress whose roles seem limited to B-movies, utterly devoid of any artistic merit. Lastly, Joey (Mary Beth Hurt) feels plagued by insecurity and seems unable to find the right career path. She craves creativity, doesn't want children but can't figure out what she does want to do. All three share a reliance on their mother's ability to design the "interiors" of their lives for them. A reliance that has left them dependent on her, without the capabilities to lead lives on their own terms.

Many viewers complain that this film is too depressing, too self-indulgent and that the characters are shallow, but morbidity is a part of our real-life experience and here Woody's characters demonstrate both shallowness *and* genuine depth. This is a mature, well-acted, realistic piece of work that, despite not taking great box office, received good reviews. Allen should be applauded for not following up the success of *Annie Hall* with what was expected of him. Of course, some fans may be put off by its slow pace

and lack of gags, but for the more curious there is much to admire and contemplate. Interestingly, *Interiors* was released in the same year as Ingmar Bergman's *Autumn Sonata*. Their content shares similarities too - a similar pacing, a bleak atmosphere and an unwillingness to give easy answers. Woody must have found it somewhat surreal to be running against his inspiration in the best screenplay categories that year.

## Manhattan (1979)

Woody Allen ended the '70s with one of his most iconic films. Once again co-written with Marshall Brickman, *Manhattan* was shot in glorious monochrome, its opening montage combining beautiful images of New York with the music of George Gershwin in a breathtaking visual love letter to the city. Today, this startling opening sequence is as well-known and admired as the movie itself. In fact, Gershwin's *Rhapsody in Blue* had inspired Woody to make the film in the first place. The choice to film in black and white (beautifully shot by Gordon Willis) was because, as

WOODY ALLEN
DIANE KEATON
MICHAEL MURPHY
MARIEL HEMINGWAY
MERYL STREEP
ANNE BYRNE

"MANHATTAN" Music by GEORGE GERSHWIN
A JACK ROLLINS-CHARLES H. JOFFE Production
Written by WOODY ALLEN and MARSHALL BRICKMAN Directed by WOODY ALLEN
Produced by CHARLES H. JOFFE Executive Producer ROBERT GREENHUT Director of Photography GORDON WILLIS
United Artists

Allen's character narrates in his opening voice-over, "New York is a city that has always and will always exist in black and white."

In 1979, Woody's beloved New York City (specifically Manhattan) was suffering something of a crisis and he appears to have responded to this by imagining a vastly improved version, a New York cast in the fantasy form of his favourite movies and lovingly remembered photographic portraits from childhood. Allen attempts to combine bittersweet comedy with his own nostalgia and a timeless romanticism... and he certainly succeeds.

Woody plays Isaac, a twice divorced writer, who is 42 but dating a 17-year-old student named Tracy (Mariel Hemingway). Neurotic Isaac is beginning to feel uncomfortable with the age difference between them and to complicate this his ex-wife (eye-catchingly played by a young Meryl Streep) is writing a book about her relationship with him. To make matters even worse, he has quit his job as a television comedy writer to write his own book but, due to growing financial worries, is already regretting this decision. Isaac's love life becomes increasingly complicated when, despite initial reservations, he begins to fall in love with Mary Wilkie (Diane Keaton), a somewhat pretentious journalist and mistress of his best friend, Yale Pollack (Michael Murphy). Impulsively, he abruptly ends his relationship with Tracy to establish his new relationship with Mary, but later regrets this decision.

Isaac's relationship with Tracy seems to have raised very few eyebrows back in 1979. Of course today this pairing remains controversial and there are undoubtedly uncomfortable moments for modern audiences. In the

film's defence, the age difference is sensitively handled, with a finale clearly demonstrating Tracy's maturity in contrast to Isaac's rather pathetic, emotionally arrested-immaturity. In addition to this, Hemingway's vulnerable portrayal helps audiences relate to her without the need for manipulation. She was rightly rewarded with an Oscar nomination for a superbly sensitive performance.

The tight script benefits from an abundance of clever dialogue and conversations that revolve around everyday dilemmas. Allen also includes several intellectual discussions on art and cinema which are often hilarious (especially for cineastes) and reward repeat viewing. But the humour never takes precedence over the drama that unfolds on screen, while the dialogue is often so realistic that it's hard to distinguish the scripted from the improvised. *Manhattan*'s screenplay stands out as one of Woody's very best.

Cinematically, this film is something of a masterpiece, confirming Allen's significant progression as a director. The ever-shifting city landscape perfectly sets the mood for everything that happens within it; never failing to supply a perfect, complementary background image. Whether it's the stunning monochromatic cinematography, the evocative Gershwin soundtrack or the smartly written dialogue (written for often unlikable and unsympathetic characters) this is a truly wonderful piece of cinema and a quintessential New York movie. *Manhattan* proved to be another big hit for Woody, yet, ever the consummate artist, he was not satisfied with his work. Allen disliked the finished cut so much that he offered to make a movie for free for United Artists if they would scrap the film and not release it, later claiming to be bewildered by its huge success, "Anything with so much praise has a hard time living up to the hype, and to me *Manhattan* fell far short." I'm sure that most fans would disagree with this assessment but nevertheless admire his humility and authentic artistic desire for perfection.

Woody Allen's incredible output during the '70s demonstrates a writer/director rapidly learning his craft and evolving film by film. By the time he had reached *Annie Hall* in 1977, Allen was hitting creative peaks achieved by very few, with *Manhattan* only cementing his status at the top of his field. It's an incredibly sustained level of both quality and quantity by one man in one decade, a filmography that any screenwriter or director worth their salt would give their eye teeth for. Today, there is a consensus among critics, other directors and writers (and many film lovers) that at least two of the fantastic movies Woody created in this decade have established themselves as bona fide masterworks of cinema. But he wasn't finished there. Incredibly, he would go on to create several more in the years that followed.

# DEVIL CHILDREN

## The Representation of Children in Horror Movies During the 1970s

by Kev Hurst

**Robert Thorn:** *I'm the one who's supposed to kill him. These are knives! He wants me to stab him! He wants me to murder a child!*

**Keith Jennings:** *It's not a child!*
(*The Omen*, 1976)

Over the decades, the depiction of a family at crisis point has been prominent in the horror genre. A trend in '70s horror films was to show a small, personal crisis - a marriage breakdown, a separation, a troubled child, etc. - proving as intense and terrifying as more abstract supernatural chills. Messed-up families can generate the same dread and fear as horror movie staples like atomic bombs, oversized monsters, or gothic figures like Dracula, the Mummy, the Wolfman and Frankenstein's creature. Many horrors in the '70s turned to current social issues for their inspiration. They explored things which happened in everyday life to everyday people, and addressed the genuine psychological fears prevalent in the decade. The reason these movies are so terrifying is that they are so real. They show fear lurking in the one place where people should feel safest - their own home. The root of the evil might be a mother, a father, a brother, a sister, a pre-teen, a little boy, even a new-born baby.

This threat from within the home is especially effective when it involves prepubescent children. In most genres, children are represented as innocent, impressionable, vulnerable, full of goodness, but the horror genre often shows them as monstrous, demonic and powerful. They are cast as the antagonists in films of this type, hence nicknames like the 'Monstrous Child' or the 'Demonic Child' sub-genre. Most depict children who possess unique special gifts, such as mind control or some sort of deadly supernatural power. They also show children being influenced by an evil force to commit heinous acts of murder. The kills are often brutal and creative. The message seems to be that children are boisterous disruptors of modern society. They bring unhappiness and pain to the adults in their life, especially their parents.

We see this in early films such as *The Bad Seed* (1956) where a young, adopted girl is revealed to be the daughter of a notorious serial killer, perhaps explaining her sociopathy by implying a hereditary reason for her behaviour. The science-fiction horror *Village of the Damned* (1960) takes place in a fictional English village Midwich, where everyone falls unconscious and, upon awaking, discover that many of their womenfolk are mysteriously and simultaneously pregnant. They give birth to coldly emotionless children with superior intellects. The infants have a very unusual appearance - striking eyes and an odd scalp structure for the boys, identical platinum blonde hair for the girls. They grow and develop at a rapid rate, and each child has a telepathic connection with the others. A prominent example of a devil child can be found in Roman Polanski's *Rosemary's Baby* (1968), in which the title character is raped and impregnated by Satan and gives birth to his monstrous offspring. Though the child isn't shown onscreen, we're able to conjure an image of it thanks to a brilliant snippet of dialogue. "What have you done to it?

What have you done to its eyes?" gives an unsettling visual clue about what lies in the child's black cot.

The 'Monstrous Child' sub-genre came to the fore during the '70s, with at least half a dozen films - probably a lot more - utilising it. Two of the most famous were *The Exorcist* (1973) and *The Omen* (1976), and I'll return to those later, but first I'd like to mention a selection of others which fit the bill.

My first port of call is a film similar to *The Bad Seed* in tone and setting. *The Other* (1972) is based on a novel of the same name by Tom Tryon, published in in 1971. It was clearly influenced by Hitchcock's *Psycho* and other psychological horror tales from the time. It is not a particularly influential movie itself, but worth mentioning as the first film of the '70s to use the 'Monstrous Child' plot device. It is well-crafted and directed by Robert Mulligan, who'd previously helmed *To Kill a Mockingbird* (1962) and *Summer of '42* (1971). *The Other* tells the story of thirteen-year-old twins named Niles and Holland Perry who live on a farm in the bucolic countryside of a small rural town. One is full of mischief, the other full of goodness. A series of horrific accidents happen, and it seems one of the twins is always close by. Is one of them responsible for the sinister goings-on?

While the focus in *The Other* is twin brothers, the 1976 American giallo/slasher *Alice, Sweet Alice* aka *Communion* flips the concept to sisters - one good, the other suspected of being evil. Brooke Shields plays Karen Spages, the younger sister, who is brutally murdered during her first communion by a small-shaped person wearing a St. Michael's raincoat and a mask. Karen's older sister Alice (Paula Sheppard) was, we learn, born out of wedlock and receives little love from her mother. She has grown up watching Karen getting all the affection and attention.

After Karen's murder, Alice falls under suspicion from those around her. Meanwhile, a series of slayings takes place, seemingly committed by the same killer dressed in the attire I mentioned earlier. Could young Alice be responsible for the bloodthirsty mayhem?

The ghastly, deranged and obscure *The Child* (1977), from Iranian director Robert Voskanian, is an example of a non-Hollywood American horror. It found itself briefly on the Video Nasties list in the UK in the early '80s. Laurel Barnett stars as Alicianne Delmar, a young woman who returns to her hometown to work at Nordon House, a run-down estate, where her job involves looking after young Rosalie Nordon (Rosalie Cole). Rosalie seems somewhat unusual and has some unfamiliar 'friends' who hang out at the graveyard. When we first see her, she is giving a kitten to one of these so-called friends. Moments later, an elderly neighbour speaks about Rosalie's strangeness and possessiveness. She mentions that Rosalie's mother spent most of her life in mental institutions until her death. Upon arriving at the estate, Alicianne meets Rosalie's father Joshua and his son Len. As the story progresses, we learn Rosalie has a terrifying secret, which is that she has a psychic ability called psychokinesis. She can control the living dead, summoning them to take revenge on everyone she thinks played a part in her mother's death. No-one is safe from her anger - neither her own family, nor anyone she deems a threat... including her new nanny.

*Who Can Kill a Child?* (1976), from Spanish director

Narcisco Ibanez Serrador, tells the story of a group of children who have killed all the adults in a small village. There are similarities here to Stephen King's short story 'Children of the Corn' and the sci-fi chiller *Village of the Damned*. In *Who Can Kill A Child?*, young English couple Tom and Evelyn (Lewis Fiander and Prunella Ransome) embark on an adventure to a secluded island off the Spanish coast. When they arrive, they are surprised to find the village almost uninhabited, apart from a large group of youngsters who appear to have taken over the town. Their behaviour is violent and very territorial. The children attack the couple, forcing them to seek sanctuary until they can figure out a way off the island. Tom and Evelyn realise some form of madness is manipulating the kids, an unnamed evil which transmits when they make eye contact with each other. There's a scene where one already murderous child walks up to an uninfected peer and locks eyes on him, and within moments, the uninfected child is under the spell of the murderous child, copying his behaviour. There is a clear social/political metaphor here,

highlighting the effect years of exposure to violence can have on children. Documentary-style footage in the early scenes shows children enduring perils throughout history. We see them during World War 2, in concentration camps; we see war crimes committed against the young, and pictures from the Vietnam War of children being routinely injured and murdered.

"There's only one thing wrong with the Davis baby…" according to B-movie auteur Larry Cohen, who wrote and directed his own 'Monster Baby' entry in 1974 titled *It's Alive*. The film features a hideous clawed and fanged mutant baby who kills the entire delivery team when being born. Soon after, the new-born conducts a wave of killings for food and shelter. The film plays on all our natural fears and uncertainties about raising children, maintaining a family unit and being a parent. At one point, the mother Lenore (Sharon Farrell) asks her husband Frank (John P. Ryan) if the arrival of a baby will make him feel trapped. It's implied they may have considered an abortion earlier in her pregnancy. Throughout the movie, we sense an underlying hatred towards children. It is reinforced everywhere through subtle signs and snippets of dialogue. Like the moment where a police officer states: "people without children don't realise how lucky they are." We also see the mutant baby stealing food and milk from the fridge, which we should interpret as a wider comment about the way children drain your resources and deplete your possessions. There's a great shot which lingers longer than

necessary on the words 'Stop Children' emblazoned on the back of a van. Interestingly, the film blames the mother herself for causing her baby's mutated appearance. She has been using birth control pills, which in the '70s were a relatively new pharmaceutical product viewed by the general public with uncertainty and suspicion.

Considered by many film scholars and critics as the 'Citizen Kane' of demonic child movies, *The Omen* (1976) follows the story of the son of the Antichrist. During a thunderous night in Rome, American diplomat Robert Thorn (Gregory Peck) deceives his wife (Lee Remick) to spare her grief after their child has died within moments of being born. He agrees to take a different child, born almost simultaneously, whose mother died while giving birth. Unbeknownst to the pair, the child they are raising is in fact the offspring of Satan himself. They name him Damien and raise him with love and devotion, little realising the deadly events which await as he grows. Damien is guarded by rottweilers which prowl constantly, ensuring his well-being. His nanny hangs herself during Damien's 5th birthday party, and a new nanny arrives unexpectedly. Mrs. Baylock (Billie Whitelaw) seems prim and efficient but is really a demon sent from hell to serve and protect Damien until his powers mature. At this early age, Damien never really

instigates evil acts; other people commit terrible acts on his behalf. When he knocks his mother over, killing her unborn child, it is actually Mrs. Baylock who opens the door allowing Damien to ride his bike from his bedroom into the stool on which his mom is standing. Later, it is revealed Damien was not born from a human womb but was in fact born from a jackal, showing that Thorn was deceived from the start by those who persuaded him to take the motherless baby as his own. In the sequel *Damien: Omen II* (1978), the titular devil child is older and more powerful, and commits several killings of his own.

The last example I'd like to cover here is *The Exorcist* (1973), William Friedkin's masterpiece based on a 1971 novel of the same name by William Peter Blatty. *The Exorcist* introduces us to a mother and daughter - Chris and Regan MacNeil (Ellen Burstyn and Linda Blair) - who live in Georgetown, Maryland. It's interesting that there doesn't seem to be a father in her life, linking back to the point I made at the start about these '70s horrors being built around small personal stories which feature broken family units. Regan is nearing the end of adolescence as the story opens, and is a typical healthy, innocent young girl. Her concerns and priorities are all completely normal - the clothes she wears, wanting to own a horse, etc. She's still at a vulnerable age where she needs and wants the love of her mother. This all changes when Regan makes contact though a Ouija board with a demon called Captain Howdy (aka Pazuzu). Soon after, she shows signs of abnormal

YOU HAVE BEEN WARNED

IF SOMETHING FRIGHTENING HAPPENS TO YOU TODAY, THINK ABOUT IT

IT MAY BE

THE OMEN

TWENTIETH CENTURY-FOX Presents

GREGORY PECK   LEE REMICK
THE OMEN
A HARVEY BERNHARD-MACE NEUFELD PRODUCTION
Co-starring DAVID WARNER   BILLIE WHITELAW
Executive Producer MACE NEUFELD   Produced by HARVEY BERNHARD   Directed by RICHARD DONNER
Written by DAVID SELTZER   Music by JERRY GOLDSMITH   PANAVISION®   Prints by DELUXE®
ORIGINAL SOUNDTRACK ALBUM ON TATTOO RECORDS AND TAPES. DISTRIBUTED BY R.C.A. RECORDS.

and often disturbing behaviour - emotional disorders, tantrums, outbursts, hurling foul profanities at doctors and houseguests and her own mother, wetting herself, attacking a psychiatrist, stabbing herself in the vaginal area

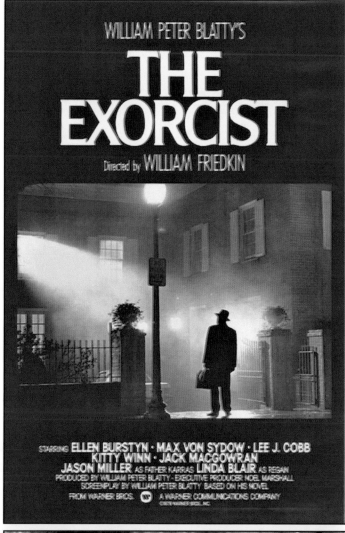

with a crucifix. Regan becomes fully monstrous, a far cry from the sweet child we first encountered. The demonic presence inside her causes havoc, driving her mother to despair.

Children are still being used often in the horror genre to this day. The '80s gave us the likes of *Children of the Corn* (1984), with an 11-year-old antagonist Isaac Chroner leading a small town's children who kill off all the adults and worship an evil deity; *Firestarter* (1984) wherein young Drew Barrymore can start fires with her mind; and *Pet Sematary* (1989) in which the reanimated corpse of Gage Creed (Miko Hughes) is possessed by the evil spirit of a Wendigo. In the '90s, the psychological horror *The Good Son* (1993) gave us Macaulay Culkin playing an evil, violent brat terrorising his cousin, and the J-horror *Ringu* (1998) presented the tale of a cursed video tape (those who have watched it being are within seven days by the vengeful spirit of a young girl called Sadako). 21st century horror has given us the Swedish vampire flick *Let the Right One In* (2008) about a twelve-year-old boy who develops a strong connection with a young girl-vampire, unhinged teenagers menacing a couple on a holiday break in *Eden Lake* (2008), a psychopathic nine-year-old girl causing mayhem in *Orphan* (2009), *Brightburn* (2019) wherein a young boy has the powers of Superman but intends to use them for evil (namely, to destroy the world), and *The Innocents* (2021), a Norwegian film featuring psychically gifted children. The list goes on. I've barely even scratched the surface.

The horror genre shows how children can be corrupted by evil, or can *be* evil themselves. It is safe to say that devilish little boys and girls are here to stay and will remain part of the horror film landscape for years to come.

*"The Wicked are estranged from the womb; they go astray as soon as they are born, speaking lies."*

Psalms 58:3

# "Dyin' ain't much of a livin'"
# THE OUTLAW JOSEY WALES

**by James Lecky**

Let's begin with a bold statement: *The Outlaw Josey Wales* is Clint Eastwood's masterpiece.

Sweeping yet intimate, grim yet humorous, violent yet redemptive, *Josey Wales* is a film that both delights in and subverts the expectations of the western.

By the mid '70s, Eastwood was a bona fide movie star, parlaying his initial European success into Hollywood (then global) recognition. The starring role in *Dirty Harry* (1971) had helped move his screen image from the rural to the urban, yet he continued (and continues) to be closely identified with the western.

Unsurprisingly, his directorial debut was the Leone-influenced *High Plains Drifter* (1973), but in the same year he also made the little seen May-to-December romance *Breezy*, starring William Holden and Kay Lenz. Eastwood

would continue to alternate between commercial and personal throughout his career, with varying degrees of success. One of his best films of the '80s, *Bronco Billy* (1980), for example, shows him at his most vulnerable, yet failed to achieve the same success as *Every Which Way But Loose* (1978) and its sequel *Any Which Way You Can* (1980), in which he jovially sent up his tough-guy persona, something which *The Outlaw Josey Wales* does more effectively and with greater subtlety.

Josey Wales, a peaceful farmer living on the Kansas-Missouri border during the American Civil War, has his home attacked and family slaughtered by Redlegs (Union Irregulars) led by Captain Terrill (Bill McKinney). Scarred but alive, he embarks upon the vengeance trail after joining 'Bloody Bill' Anderson (John Russell) and his southern guerrillas. He learns to shoot and kill with single-minded efficiency. At the war's end, refusing to surrender and betrayed by the Union Government, who massacre his comrades, he drifts south toward Texas with the authorities on his trail. Along the way he encounters numerous enemies but more importantly several allies, including elderly Cherokee chief Lone Watie (Chief Dan George), Little Moonlight (Geraldine Keams), Grandma Sarah Turner (Paula Trueman) and her granddaughter, the waifish Laura Lee (Sondra Locke), two Kansas 'pilgrims' and a mangy red-bone hound. Collectively they form an ersatz clan and gradually help him to find both peace and love again.

Almost from the word go, *The Outlaw Josey Wales* inverts the revenge theme. In most revenge westerns (and various thrillers, for that matter) the Wronged Man sets out to find the villains and dispense his own brand of justice, but here Josey is the one being pursued, and his revenge upon Bill McKinney's scowling Redleg Captain Terrill is an almost incidental catharsis, albeit one very pleasing to the audience.

Even as it faltered as a commercial genre, the American western enjoyed an artistic renaissance and *The Outlaw Josey Wales* sits with some remarkable examples of the form. 1972 alone saw the release of Robert Aldrich's *Ulzana's Raid*, Mark Rydell's *The Cowboys*, Robert Benton's *Bad Company*, Sydney Pollack's *Jeremiah Johnson* and Dick

Richards' *The Culpepper Cattle Company*. Added to these should be the elegiac *Pat Garrett and Billy the Kid* (1973) and Don Siegel's *The Shootist* (1976), films which lament the loss of the western itself.

The influence of Sergio Leone and Don Siegel on Eastwood as a filmmaker has been noted before but is still well worth mentioning. From one he had learned scale and scope, from the other a brisk efficiency which enhanced rather than hampered his work. Leone and Siegel had helped to make Eastwood an icon, to the extent where knowing nods to his on-screen persona could be dropped into the World War II crime romp *Kelly's Heroes* (1970) and the catchphrase "Do you feel lucky, punk?" has entered the lexicon of an entire generation.

*The Outlaw Josey Wales* saw him return to the western four years after *Joe Kidd*, a film which promised much - helmed as it was by John Sturges, director of *The Magnificent Seven* and the minor classic *The Law and Jake Wade* - but was ultimately a little lacklustre. There was a sense that, in his westerns at least, Eastwood was marking

time. If so, it was time well spent, for his return to the form would be not only one of the finest westerns of the '70s but one of the finest of all time.

Eastwood's star status allowed him a certain leverage when it came to choosing his collaborators, and to direct *The Outlaw Josey Wales* he turned to screenwriter Philip Kaufman who had made *The Great Northfield Minnesota Raid* (1972) a film which - perhaps not unnaturally - shares a great deal with *Josey Wales*, at least in its initial setup, Both concern unreconstructed rebels and both have cast members in common including Matt Clark, Royal Dano and Madeleine Taylor Holmes, the latter memorable as Granny Hawkins ("They say you're a hard put and desperate man, Josey Wales. They're goin' to heel and hide you to a barn door. You know what I say? I say that big talk's worth doodly-squat.")

Both films also share a certain autumnal look during the Kansas-Missouri sequences (courtesy of the cinematography of Bruce Surtees, a frequent Eastwood collaborator) and the question of how much influence Kaufman had on *Josey Wales* might be asked since he had co-written the screenplay with Sonia Chernus and he and Eastwood worked closely together prior to the beginning of principal photography.

A rift quickly developed between the two, fuelled by that age old catch all 'artistic differences'. Kaufman's meticulous approach did not sit well with Eastwood, and the rumours that both men had romantic designs on Sondra Locke probably didn't help matters. Regardless, Kaufman was fired after a few weeks of filming with Eastwood taking the helm (an incident which led to the creation of the Eastwood Rule, prohibiting an actor or producer from taking control in similar circumstances).

It is, of course, somewhat pointless to speculate on what Philip Kaufman's *The Outlaw Josey Wales* might or might not have been since the film belongs, magnificently, to Clint Eastwood.

Hollywood has always had a fascination with unrepentant outlaws, often turning them into Robin Hood figures (then happily deconstructing them as fashion dictates). Jesse James has been incarnated on-screen by a diverse range of actors including Tyrone Power, Robert Wagner, Audie Murphy, Robert Duvall, James Keach and Brad Pitt, while Billy the Kid has been portrayed by Paul Newman, Marlon Brando (at least in spirit in *One Eyed Jacks* [1961]), Michael J. Pollard, Kris Kristofferson and Emilio Estevez. And, of course, the titular characters of George Roy Hill's *Butch Cassidy and the Sundance Kid* were presented as folk heroes.

Josey Wales sits easily in the midst. In general, the Hollywood outlaw-hero is a wronged man: sometimes by officialdom, sometimes by the western equivalent of Big Business (corrupt ranchers and land barons), but always beset by forces greater than he.

*The Outlaw Josey Wales* is essentially a picaresque tale - one which bears comparison with Leone's *The Good, the Bad and the Ugly* (1966). Both are episodic in their narrative, but whereas Leone's film has a definite goal in mind for its protagonists (a hidden cache of gold), the ultimate goals of the characters in *Josey Wales* are much more nebulous and, in a sense, more valuable. They yearn after freedom, in whatever form it might take. For Grandma Sarah and Laura Lee, it is represented by the ranch left abandoned by Sarah's son, Tom. For Lone Watie and Little Moonlight, it is a chance to live how they choose, unfettered by outside interference. And for Josey Wales himself, it is a chance, however remote, to leave violence behind (a point underscored in the scene where he tells a would-be bounty hunter (John Davis Chandler) "Dyin' ain't much of a livin', boy.")

Like *The Good, the Bad and the Ugly*, the narrative moves across the landscape and allows for some spectacular and violent set-pieces. Like that film and regardless of its many, many virtues, *The Outlaw Josey Wales* is essentially an action film, or at least, a film with action at its heart.

Josey himself is practically a one-man army, laden with pistols and rifles, but as quick with his wits as he is with his guns ("Well, Mr. Carpetbagger. We got somethin' in this territory called the Missouri *boat ride*"), yet Eastwood never allows the film's violence to become its central message, balancing it with a strong and pervasive sense of humour.

Much of the heart is provided by Chief Dan George as Lone Watie, a dispossessed Cherokee who becomes Josey's unlikely sidekick. As legend has it, the 77-year-old actor (who had risen to prominence in Arthur Penn's *Little Big Man* [1970]) had difficulty learning the lines as scripted, so Eastwood encouraged him to simply tell the story in his own words leading to a performance of humour, depth and sensitivity far removed from the usual portrayal of Native Americans in most westerns up to this point.

But Lone Watie is not the only character who brings a touch of lightness to what might other have been a singularly grim undertaking. Several Eastwood regulars turn up in supporting parts including Woodrow Parfrey as an oily carpetbagger happily selling snake oil to the gullible ("This is it... one dollar a bottle. It works wonders on wounds." "Works wonders on just about everything, eh?" "It can do 'most anything." "How is it with stains?") and William O'Connell as the ferryman Sim Carstairs - "in my line of work, you gotta be able to sing either *The Battle Hymn of the Republic* or *Dixie* with equal enthusiasm. . . dependin' upon present company" - while John Quade turns up as a vicious Comanchero leader.

A particular note should be made of John Vernon who had previously appeared with Eastwood in *Dirty Harry* as the Mayor and, memorably, opposite Lee Marvin in John Boorman's *Point Blank* (1967). As Fletcher, he is the one who persuades the remnants of Bloody Bill's guerrillas to surrender, only to find himself betrayed by the duplicitous Senator Lane (Frank Schofield), forced to witness the massacre of his comrades then tasked with hounding Wales to kingdom come. Vernon's character - the only one other than Josey himself to encompass the entire narrative - is never allowed to be simply a villain and, in the end, plays his own part in Josey's redemption ("I think I'll try to tell him the war is over. What do you say? . . " "I reckon so. I guess we all died a little in that damn war.")

Eastwood, naturally, has his fair share of quips and one-liners, mostly delivered in his trademark growl, ("Hell with them fellas, buzzard's gotta eat same as worms") but there is never a sense that as star/director he allows himself to hog the limelight or the camera. Rather, he (or rather Josey) is the centre of the film, but certain scenes, or their aftermath, see the character somewhat sidelined in order to allow the supporting actors to shine, and he is never afraid to be the butt of the joke when necessary. At one point he is assisted in a four-on-one gunfight by Lone Watie ("Never paid him no mind, you were there." "I might have missed.") and, later, a stern rebuke from Grandma Sarah forces him to swallow a mouthful of tobacco juice rather than indulge in his trademark spit with which he often punctuates a moment.

For better or worse, Eastwood's western characters will always be compared with The Man with No Name (aka Joe, Manco and Blondie) but Josey Wales is a much more complex character. To begin with, Josey is not simply a wandering Stranger. We are allowed to glimpse his life prior to the violence and are left in no doubt about his origins and motivations, nor is he as self-serving as his European incarnation - in the title sequence he is seen ministering to a dying Bloody Bill; later, he breaks off a murderous gunfight with the hated Redlegs, not to protect his own life but to save that of the wounded Jamie (Sam Bottoms); he reluctantly rescues Little Moonlight from a life of servitude and abuse; attacks a band of Comancheros in order to save Grandma Sarah and Laura Lee; and, in one of the most memorable scenes, parlays with the Comanche Chief Ten Bears (Will Sampson), offering words of Life or Death: "I came here to die with you. Or to live with you. Dying ain't so hard for men like you and me. It's living that's hard when all you've ever cared about has been butchered or raped."

Behind the camera, Eastwood's direction is fluid and assured. Even the landscape of the film changes to reflect character. Lush and green in the pre-title sequence, moving from muted browns into snow specked scenes then hard desert before coming practically full circle at the Santa Rio ranch with its promise of peace and plenty. One senses a deep understanding of how cinema works - very often, looks convey more than words, costume adds depth to minor roles (Woodrow Parfrey's carpetbagger, for example, whose various indignities are compounded by the white suit he wears, or John Davis Chandler as the doomed bounty hunter whose honour won't let him walk away). Music is used expertly to enhance the moving image.

Like the film itself, Jerry Fielding's score is never content to rest upon its laurels or rely too overtly on previous westerns. It changes mood with the landscape and characters, near-bombastic when it needs to be, dynamic in the action scenes, haunting in the tender moments.

As a side note, it would be remiss to ignore a minor controversy which accompanied the release of *The Outlaw Josey Wales*. It was based upon the novel 'The Rebel Outlaw Josey Wales' (later retitled 'Gone to Texas') by Forrest Carter, a supposed Cherokee storyteller. The revelations that Carter was, in fact, Asa Earl Carter - a Klansman and white supremacist - threatened to taint the production. Carter was also rumoured to be a nightmare in real life, so the film quietly distanced itself from him.

While *Unforgiven* (1992) deservedly won many awards, including the all-important Best Picture Oscar, *The Outlaw Josey Wales* marked Eastwood as a director of importance, not merely an actor with pretensions behind the camera. It shows a filmmaker at the height of his powers, artistically and commercially.

The legendary Orson Welles said that: "it [*Josey Wales*] belongs with the great westerns of Ford and Hawks and people like that."

High praise indeed. And well deserved.

# THE MIDNIGHT MAN

## An Adult Motion Picture

**Dr. Andrew C. Webber suggests the shadow of *Chinatown* hangs heavy over 1974.**

It's interesting to note that during the '70s a significant number of American film stars turned director. Far and away the most successful of the bunch was Clint Eastwood, who turned in *Play Misty for Me, Breezy, High Plains Drifter, The Eiger Sanction, The Outlaw Josey Wales* and *The Gauntlet* during the decade. Woody Allen was up there, too.

And there were others - Jack Lemmon made *Kotch* (1971), featuring a brilliant performance from his old mate Walter Matthau; Robert Culp made the underrated *Hickey and Boggs* (1972) from a script by Walter Hill; Kirk Douglas directed and starred in two westerns - *Scalawag* (1973), a re-telling of 'Treasure Island' set in the Wild West, and the pretty good *Posse* (1975); Burt Reynolds worked on both sides of the camera for *Gator* (1976) and *The End* (1978); Warren Beatty co-directed the smash hit *Heaven Can Wait*, aided by Buck Henry, in 1978.

And, in 1974, Burt Lancaster - who had previously directed *The Kentuckian* (1955) - made *The Midnight Man*. His second stab at directing (co-helmed by its scriptwriter Roland Kibbee) is a taut, overlooked neo-noir with an interesting cast and something to say about the death of the American Dream. It is based on David Anthony's novel 'The Midnight Lady and the Mourning Man'.

Co-director and writer Kibbee had regularly collaborated with Burt - he'd contributed to, amongst others, *The Crimson Pirate, Vera Cruz* and *Valdez is Coming*. Harold Hecht (who was a partner in the Hecht-Hill-Lancaster production company) had identified Kibbee as

a communist during the McCarthy-era HUAC witch-hunt. Kibbee and Hecht subsequently fell out, though Kibbee and Lancaster remained on friendly terms. They set up Norlan Productions together to produce *The Midnight Man*.

The tagline - "The Ex-Con, the Hippie, the Senator, the Pervert, the Lesbian, the Professor, The Sheriff, the Sadist: one of them is a murderer" - gives a flavour of what to expect from this downbeat movie. Its glum style would be seen again in Arthur Penn's *Night Moves* (1975) and Robert Aldrich's *Hustle* (1975), two further films which lift the lid off the seedy underbelly of society while (in the true mid '70s style of frank language, bloody violence and explicit sexual references) depicting previously unmentionable evils like child abuse and incest at their stinking heart. Undeniably, there's a hung-over feeling to these films stemming from the legacy of Vietnam, Nixon's presidency, Watergate and the oil crisis. The relative failure of the peace-and-love generation to fully break down the taboos and restrictions of their parents' values hovers in the background. Businessmen are shown to be corrupt. Teachers, politicians and cops are not to be trusted. Everyone's in it for themselves, and the drugs (by now harder and more addictive) definitely don't work.

Other films from 1974 with a similarly cynical and pessimistic worldview include *Bring Me the Head of Alfredo Garcia, Busting, California Split, Cockfighter, The Conversation, Death Wish, Foxy Brown, Freebie and the Bean, The Gambler,*

The Klansman, Mr Majestyk, Newman's Law, The Parallax View, Report to the Commissioner, The Sugarland Express, The Taking of Pelham 123 and Thunderbolt and Lightfoot. All are mid-priced, modern-day thrillers. Many of them end ambiguously or bleakly. Their downbeat denouements definitely make them appealing and unusual compared with today's movies. Few films nowadays are as bent on reflecting what's going on in the wider world or capturing the audience's collective mood of despair, frustration and paranoia. The shadow of Chinatown (released a few months after The Midnight Man) hangs heavy over the cinematic landscape of 1974, that's for sure.

It was, moreover, a year of boundary-pushing sleaze - The Night Porter and The Texas Chainsaw Massacre were also big hits and played their parts in cinema becoming more permissive. The Midnight Man has its fair share of bad language, pornography, bloodletting and sex. Unsurprisingly, perhaps, the biggest hits of the year were the disaster movies Earthquake, Airport 75 and The Towering Inferno, as if that genre somehow captured a sense of the impending doom and danger that lurked in America's now defunct dream.

Lancaster had made his debut in Robert Siodmak's terrific noir The Killers (1946). He was one of the few big stars from the golden age who'd managed to sustain his career into the '70s. He began the decade with Airport, a big hit, the daddy of the disaster cycle, and followed it with a trio of impressive revisionist westerns: Michael Winner's Lawman, Valdez is Coming (with Susan Clark, who co-stars here) and Aldrich's Vietnam parable Ulzana's Raid (Aldrich

had helped consolidate Lancaster's status as a big star in *Apache* and *Vera Cruz* in 1954, and they would go on to work together again on *Twilight's Last Gleaming* in 1977). Just before *The Midnight Man*, Lancaster re-teamed with Michael Winner for the plodding Euro spy drama *Scorpio* and the paranoid JFK conspiracy thriller *Executive Action*. Lancaster was a liberal who opposed the Vietnam War and the death penalty, and his pessimism about mid '70s America pervades every aspect of *The Midnight Man*, his second (and last) film as director.

He plays Jim Slade, a hard-bitten ex-con (and former cop), the lowest of the low, eking out his new-found freedom as a night watchman at a smalltown college campus (the film was shot in South Carolina and set in the fictional town of Jordon). An attractive co-ed, played by debutant Catherine Bach (later seen in *Hustle* but best known for playing Daisy Duke in TV's *The Dukes of Hazzard*), winds up dead and the subsequent investigation unearths various ugly secrets.

Lancaster had been playing flawed characters as far back as *The Sweet Smell of Success* (1957), through a number of '60s movies like *Elmer Gantry*, *Seven Days in May*, *The Swimmer* and *The Gypsy Moths*. Here, he turns in a sombre performance as Slade, a man attempting to redeem himself after shooting his wife's lover when he found them in bed together. This shot at redemption takes place against the

backdrop of an unforgiving world, where no-one is to be trusted and everyone seems out to get him. He's the kind of guy who goes to the movies alone and smokes a solitary cigarette afterwards (if you look closely, you can see the "forthcoming attraction" at the local movie theatre is Phil Kaufman's 1972 western *The Great Northfield Minnesota Raid*).

Canadian Susan Clark plays Lancaster's love interest, but is also "the lesbian" referred to in the tagline. She was an also-ran actress who happened to appear in some good movies in the '70s, like cult sci-fi entry *Colossus - The Forbin Project*, *Skin Game* (a slave trade comedy-western starring James Garner and Lou Gossett which pre-dates Tarantino's *Django Unchained* by almost 40 years), Arthur Penn's *Night Moves* and the Sherlock Holmes meets Jack the Ripper thriller *Murder by Decree*. Here, she is given a central and duplicitous role as Slade's parole officer. She brings a cold sexuality to the part, especially in the finale where she casually parades before him in her bra, revealing just how foolish he has been to be taken in by her.

Whatever its faults (especially the ill-advised voiceover near the climax), *The Midnight Man* boasts a number of memorable character actors in small roles who really leave their mark - another thing you don't see much in modern Hollywood offerings.

Sleepy-eyed Harris Yulin, who plays the corrupt sheriff, possesses a very interesting and memorable face. He usually played reptilian scumbags, and his role here is a prototype for most parts which followed, most notably in *Night Moves*. The less familiar Cameron Mitchell plays Lancaster's best friend Quartz - like so many interesting American actors, he'd end up plying his trade in low-budget, often dreadful horror fare like *The Toolbox Murders* (1978) and Sergio Martino's *Island of the Fishmen* (1979) alongside the likes of Joseph Cotten, Richard Johnson and former Bond girl Barbara Bach. Ed Lauter, last seen alongside Lancaster in *Executive Action*, is reliable in almost everything and is one of the great '70s supporting actors. Here, he plays Leroy, member of a weird hillbilly family who get drawn into the affair ("He's ma meat," he yells threateningly, before laying into Lancaster). Charles Tyner, another very familiar face, plays the misogynistic and hypocritical underwear-collecting janitor ("damned whores!" he whines), a prime suspect if ever there was one. Robert Quarry plays a suspicious teacher, Dr Prechette. Quarry, like Cameron Mitchell, would find himself pigeon-holed as a horror actor after being cast as Count Yorga in 1971 (in the following year he appeared in *Dr. Phibes Rises Again*). This is a rare dramatic role for him and he delivers a suitably smarmy performance, similar to the work he did on *Rollercoaster* (1977). Bill Lancaster, Burt's blonde son, plays "the Hippie." He shares a couple of scenes with his dad, which are nicely performed. Interestingly, before an untimely death from a heart attack at the age of 49, Bill managed to find the time to write screenplays for *The Bad News Bears* (1976) and John Carpenter's *The Thing* (1982). Finally, a South Carolina politician with the unlikely name Weems Oliver Baskin III can be seen in a small cameo as a bartender (his nose is especially memorable).

Along with *The Godfather Part II*, *The Midnight Man*

would have been one of the last films to be printed in Technicolor (an enormously expensive process which enhanced colours but demanded more lighting and used a complex, costly dye-transfer system in the print processing stages). The colour red is used to luscious effect throughout, giving depth and richness to Jack Priestley's cinematography (he'd also shot Anthony Quinn in *Across 110th Street* and Ivan Passer's junkie drama *Born to Win* with George Segal, Karen Black, Paula Prentiss and a very young Robert De Niro).

The film is edited by Frank Morriss, who had worked on Siegel's superb *Charley Varrick*.

The soundtrack is provided by Dave Grusin, aiming for a ragged '70s wah-wah sound. The catchy title song *Come Back Where You Belong* (which, if you listen to the lyrics, serves as one of the movie's key clues) is sung by Yvonne Elliman, recently seen in Norman Jewison's musical *Jesus Christ Superstar*.

Burt didn't like the film - and it made no money. After directing it, he was a *changed* man. He made amends by working with directorial giants like Luchino Visconti on *Conversation Piece*, Bernardo Bertolucci on the epic *Novocento* (alongside Robert De Niro, Gerald Depardieu and Donald Sutherland), and Robert Altman on *Buffalo Bill and the Indians* (a rare misfire, in spite of its starry cast including Paul Newman, Harvey Keitel, Joel Grey, Geraldine Chaplin and Will Sampson).

Did something happen whilst making *The Midnight Man* which subsequently caused him to seek out such auteurs to work with? Who knows? Burt may not have liked it, but for fans of dark, occasionally depressing mid '70s dramas which represent America as a broken land, there's much to enjoy in this taut, intelligent and undervalued minor murder mystery.

*The Midnight Man* is definitely a late-night treat.

# The Family as a Nation
# THE CEREMONY

by Bryan C. Kuriawa

Much like their contemporaries in France and the United States, Japanese filmmakers experienced their own cinematic New Wave in the post-war era. The inaugural point for this was the mid '50s, with Nikkatsu Studios releasing their 'Sun Tribe' films which were stories of bored, rebellious youths. Director Yasuzo Masumura at rival company Daiei would question modern business ethics in multiple productions, including *Giants and Toys* (1958) and *Black Test Car* (1962).

At the Shochiku Company, an up-and-coming director named Nagisa Ōshima was assigned to work on such projects. He initially mirrored the 'Sun Tribe' outings about rebellious individuals, but soon he began to push political buttons. His 1960 film *Night and Fog in Japan* was a direct indictment of the nation's political left and the 1952 security treaty with the United States.

Frustrated within the confines of the studio system, Oshima formed his own company called Sozo-Sha. His only encounters with Shochiku were when they distributed his new films theatrically. Embracing the political movements of the decade, he used the ideals of German theater director Bertolt Brecht to critique Japanese society. In 1971, this would lead to the last triumph of the Japanese New Wave - his film *The Ceremony*.

### "And Finally It Was In Japan That We Were Arrested By The Japanese"

Masuo Sakurada (Kenzo Kawarasaki), a high school baseball coach, is facing an unusual situation. He's received a telegram from his cousin, Terumichi (Atsuo Nakamura).

The subject of the message is Terumichi's own impending death. Masuo has not seen his cousin since he cut ties with his recently deceased grandfather, Kazuomi (Kei Sato), eight years previously.

Knowing his cousin lives on a remote island at the southernmost tip of Japan, he needs to learn the truth. Travelling with his only other cousin, Ritsuko (Atsuko Kaku), he plans to find out. While Ritsuko insists that they are only relatives, Masuo has deeper feelings.

On the train and boat ride, Masuo begins recalling his experiences with the Sakurada family. Returning to Japan in 1947 from Manchuria, his mother had no interest in her deceased husband's family. Masuo's father had returned to Japan two years prior, but committed suicide on New Year's Day 1946. Despite her requests, Kazuomi adopts them into his family and plans to help Masuo with his education.

Meeting Terumichi, Ritsuko and Tadashi (Kiyoshi Tsuchiya), the tour are viewed as the continuation of the family. Ritsuko's mom, Satsuko (Akiko Koyama), who cared much for Masuo's father, has an overactive interest in her nephew. Over the next 16 years, and several events, the façade of this respected local family begins to crack.

A controversial and blunt look at Japan via a family, *The Ceremony* is one of Ōshima's best films. By deconstructing his country in such a manner, he presents the uncertainty of post-war Japan and the uneasy future that lay ahead.

### "Leader of a Wave"

Often compared to the French filmmaker Jean-Luc

Godard, Ōshima was viewed as the center of Japan's New Wave. He was a director who, like Masumura, Mashiro Shinoda, Shohei Imamura, Hiroshi Teshigahara and Koji Wakamatsu, critiqued Japan's new culture. A recurring theme of each of these filmmakers was the topic of identity, specifically what was their nation's identity after suffering wartime defeat?

Teshigahara would focus on this the most, especially in his 1964 Academy-Award winner *Woman in The Dunes*. Yet it was his later outing *The Man Without a Map* (1968) which was more direct in this outlook, spotlighting a nameless private investigator (Shintaro Katsu) who searches for a woman's missing husband but is increasingly unable to made headway. While not a great film, its overall tone asks an important question - were individuals so interchangeable in this new Japan that they could vanish without trace?

What about the political side of this subject? Many of the New Wavers leaned to the radical left in their views. Ōshima had made Japan's orthodox political left the subject of numerous critiques in past films. Even so, Wakamatsu's 1969 film *Running in Madness, Dying in Love* spotlighted the futility of radical political conduct. Showcasing a young activist (Ken Yoshizawa), who runs away with his sister-in-law (Yoko Muto), they're forced to return to his brother (Kokko Toura) at the end of their journey. The final shot of him, looking for them after their reunion, represents the dead end of his radicalism.

By 1971, the Japanese New Wave was coming to an end as their outlook transitioned to newer forms and topics. Into this world, Ōshima's production takes the subject of national identity and grafts it onto a family.

## "*I Like These Ceremonies Because Lots of Things Happen*"

Performance-wise, each of the leads in *The Ceremony* succeeds in exemplifying the themes of Ōshima's critique.

As Masuo, Kawarasaki presents a very melancholy and depressing figure. Narrating over the film's events, he critiques how he was absorbed into his father's family. Separated from his mother, he enjoyed playing baseball, but gave up the sport after her death in 1952. Increasingly obsessed over the blurred lines in his family, he develops unhealthy traits. His aunt fawns over him and he has a desire for her, while also having a crush on his cousin, Ritsuko. Incest is not only implied, but seemingly encouraged, within this structure. All this culminates in a depressing spectacle.

In 1963, when his bride fails to show up for their wedding, Masuo is devastated. Not wanting to lose face in front of the invited guests and local dignitaries, Kazuomi orders the ceremony to proceed. Going through the elaborately staged event, Masuo is broken. The only one who urges him to stop is his cousin, Tadashi, who is himself ejected

from the wedding. Breaking down afterwards, he attacks his grandfather, while family members look on.

As Terumichi, Nakamura is another standout. Most well-known as Scott Glenn's rival in John Frankenheimer's *The Challenge* (1982), his is another tragic arc. Often spoken about poorly by older relatives, he is projected by his grandfather to be Masuo's rival. Despite appearing loyal to his grandfather, even serving as his personal secretary, he harbors resentment. In 1947, after first meeting Masuo, he discharges bug spray on his relatives while shouting he must "disinfect Japan." Later on, as Masuo is berated by his grandfather after the ill-fated brideless wedding, he tells Masuo to attack his granddad. Abandoning the family, while Masuo learns his cousin's birth history, Terumichi flees to a remote island in Southern Japan.

Kaku's Ritsuko is an interesting foil for the two male leads. Due to the lack of boundaries, she's encouraged to stay within the family. Masuo harbors romantic feelings for her, as he did for her mother, yet she loves Terumichi. At their uncle's wedding in 1956, all three lie on a Shikibuton floor mattress. While Masuo lies on his stomach, the other two lay next to one another. Leaving to speak to Setsuko, he returns to find them sleeping together. At his wedding, Masuo indicates he wants to experience his first wedding night with a woman. Ritsuko remarks to him how she's already had hers. In the film's present-day of 1971, she complains to Masuo that he isn't damned and only wants to be. She also makes it clear that if Terumichi is dead, she will join him in a double suicide.

Rounding out the four leads is Tsuchiya as Tadashi. The only one of the three to have their father, he is nonetheless distant from him. His father Susumu (Fumio Watanabe) was captured by communist forces in China at the end of the war. Forced through the nightmare of a Maoist reeducation camp for a decade, he is unwilling to talk to his son. He is ignored by his family and mocked by his communist brother Isamu (Hosei Komatsu), and this affects Tadashi. Drawn towards violence, he wants to take his anger out on others and society. Becoming a loyal policeman and hardline nationalist, he is ejected from Masuo's wedding for attempting to read out his manifesto. Struck by a car that same day, he is due to be buried soon after. As Masuo cries over his wedding, Susumu similarly cries while reading out what his son wrote.

### "How I Longed to Hear That Uproar. But Where Will It Lead?"

Director Ōshima divides his scenes between the flashbacks and the journey to Terumichi's island.

The flashbacks are geared around formalism and order. Everyone is well-positioned and shown respect, even if the circumstances are less so. Masuo crying in the center of his mother's funeral while everyone else focuses on personal matters, and the uncomfortable moments of his

uncle's wedding are the standout segments.

In contrast, the present-day scenes have an informal closeness. Masuo and Ritsuko are often very near each other in the same frame. It's less restricted and presents them more as two lost figures, especially in long shots. The formal tone only returns briefly when they arrive at Terumichi's cabin and enter. Elaborately colored, it's reminiscent of Masaki Kobayashi's *Kwaidan* (1964) and is an excellent set piece.

This all creates a very controlled environment, greatly enhanced by support from Daiei Studios' Kyoto branch. The result is spaces where instability, lies and distortions lay beneath the surface despite the order and controls.

### "*Is Your Communism About Giving Communal Birth?*"

Beneath the family drama, Ōshima's film challenges the topic of Japan's identity crisis and its future.

Superbly portrayed by Kei Sato, Kazuomi is an all-controlling force. Wanting to present the ideal family, he directly involves himself in the individual lives and aspects of every family member. His xenophobic and elitist nature leads to him resorting to incest, degradation and even taking on a mistress, while exiling his wife for a short time. When Setsuko attempts to give Masuo his father's last will, she is scolded by Kazuomi, who then sexually assaults her along with Terumichi. Kazuomi refers to this as a lesson.

Within the family, his authority is absolute and all-imposing. He lives with his mistress when Masuo first arrives in Japan, but lets his wife return to him after Masuo's mom's funeral. His communist son Isamu tries

to confront his father about the incest but is dismissed. Isamu acts as Ōshima's stooge in critiquing Japan's political left. A member of the Japanese Communist Party, he defends Stalinist Russia in the '40s and later Maoist China when mocking his brother. In 1963, when dealing with Masuo's breakdown and behavior, he demands his nephew act proper like a stereotypical conservative. Constant revisionism is an ardent trait of his politics and behavior, but he's unable to effectively critique or denounce his father's conduct.

Despite being classified as a war criminal, Kazuomi is allowed to return to public life working for a state organization. His demand for total subordination for collective appearances leads to Masuo's wedding spectacle, the death of Tadashi and the collapse of the Sakurada family. His final scene shows him solemnly crying in a darkened room as Masuo looks on.

Masuo remarks in an earlier scene about how he and Ritsuko were repatriated from Manchuria, considered a great regret by some Japanese. To that end, he calls himself a "child of regret." Much like Japan itself, he is left in uncertain waters.

His grandfather's demand for obedience stifles everyone. The political left of his uncle is impotent, the right of his cousin is ignored. He, like Japan, is truly adrift. The final scene of an anguished Masuo on his cousin's island, wandering its coast, is the ultimate personification of this impasse.

His family is broken, his cousins are gone, and he must chart a new course. The older members want him to become head of the Sakurada family, but he sees no value

US disc presentation.

In the mid 2000s, there was an attempt to bring it, and other unavailable Japanese New Wave titles, to overseas film buffs. Spearheaded by Mike White, writer and former publisher of the 'Cashiers du Cinemart' filmzine, *The Ceremony* was among the titles they fansubbed and made available from their website JapaneseNewWave.com on DVD. Unfortunately, disputes over multiple issues led to them ending the website.

The movie would eventually be picked up by Janus Films/The Criterion Collection several years later. At present, it is available from their streaming website, TheCriterionChannel.com, complemented by a video in which Richard Linklater discusses the movie.

Overall, *The Ceremony* is an excellent deconstruction of post-war Japan, directly challenging the ambiguous status of the nation itself. While Ōshima was a man of the political left, this message could apply to any political distinction in his nation. In an era where Japan has to face the challenges of an aging populace, economic uncertainty and a resurgent China, the topic of 'What is Japan?' is one that needs to be at the forefront. Rather than a crippled structure that can't function, it needs to face the uncertainty and stop thinking in the past.

in older, obsolete forms. Recalling a moment of everyone playing baseball in 1947, he finds a baseball before placing his head to the shore. As his mother and he left Manchuria, they left behind his dead baby brother who he thought was buried alive. Subsequently, he puts his head to the ground trying to listen for him, despite it being impossible.

The final shot of him, with his head to the rocks, implies he may be unable to chart this new path alone and will forever be trapped in the past.

### "*For a Japanese Person, What is a Ceremony?*"

Premiering at the Cannes Film Festival in May 1971, *The Ceremony* was released in Japan by the Art Theater Guild, a company who presented multiple New Wave films. It was a success and would sweep that year's Kinema Jumpo Awards, including being their selection for Best Film of 1971.

Released in the US in 1974, Ōshima's film has long been absent from Western home video audiences. Excluding a 2015 French DVD release, there has been no British or

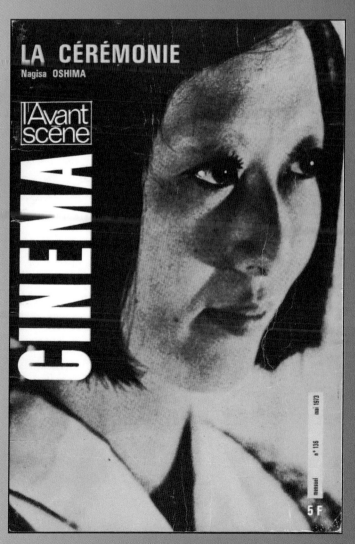

79

# THE WILD GEESE

**by Simon J. Ballard**

In cinema, the ethos tends to be: "That film went rather well, let's make our own." In the wake of the 1972 eco-horror *Frogs*, the decade was awash with similar fare such as the same year's *Night of the Lepus*, *Grizzly* (1976), *Day of the Animals* (1977) and any number of killer bee-movies. Oh, and that one with the shark, which itself spawned a host of imitators like Joe Dante's *Piranha* (1978). On the disaster front, ships tipped over, towers caught fire, the earth quaked and airplanes ran into four separate maydays. Similarly, Euan Lloyd's love of the 1961 war feature *The Guns of Navarone* begat his 1978 production *The Wild Geese* (with *Where Eagles Dare* [1968] playing its own part in this impetus). The story came from a then-unpublished novel entitled 'The Thin White Line' by Rhodesian Daniel Carney, a member of the British South African Police.

Before going into that story, I must confess I'm not a huge follower of the war genre generally, though I intend to redress this in the future. I came to *The Wild Geese* simply because it was one of my dad's favourites. I bought him the video for his birthday over twenty years ago and found myself curious to know what he loved about it. Yeah, I soon got it! Also, I mainly write horror - be it fiction or non-fiction - and my dad isn't a fan of that genre. So in writing this article about one his favourites, I feel I'm producing something he can actually read and (hopefully) enjoy. No pressure in the slightest!

Carney's manuscript had a clear message - that white and black Africans could only find peace by uniting. At the time of *The Wild Geese*, internal resistance to apartheid was becoming more militant, student demonstrations led to many deaths, and gradual reforms began to appear into the '80s.

The story concerns Colonel Allen Faulkner (Richard Burton) who arrives in London for a meeting with merchant banker Sir Edward Matherson (Stewart Granger). A former British Army officer turned mercenary, Faulkner is tasked with rescuing Julius Limbani (Winston Ntshona), the toppled president of an African nation now imprisoned and awaiting execution by General Ndofa. Faulkner recruits forty-nine fellow mercenaries, including many he has previously fought with, such as Captain Rafer Janders (Richard Harris) and Lieutenant Shawn Fynn (Roger Moore). He also hires Lieutenant Pieter Coetzee (Hardy Kruger), a former soldier in the South African Defence Force who just wants to make enough money to buy his own farm. I hardly need go into detail about the merits of this renowned bunch. Indeed, it was enough for the posters to proclaim: "Burton, Moore, Harris, Kruger are... *The Wild Geese*."

The situation here was based on an attempted coup d'état by Thomas 'Mad Mike' Hoare, a British mercenary who was hired as a technical advisor on the film. The onscreen mayhem matched his operation in 1961 Katanga, a province attempting to detach itself from the newly independent Congo Republic.

Reginald Rose, an American who wrote on a number of political and social issues, was tasked by Lloyd to write the screenplay. He had previously written the play 'Twelve Angry Men' and its 1957 film adaptation, winning an Emmy for the former and an Oscar nomination for the latter. Rose would go on to write more scripts for Lloyd - see *The Sea Wolves* (1980), *Who Dares Wins* (1982) and *Wild*

*Geese II* (1985).

It was also Lloyd's choice to hire Andrew V. McLaglen as director. A British-born American, McLaglen was noted for a string of westerns mostly featuring John Wayne or James Stewart. He began his career in television with series like *Gunsmoke, Rawhide* and *Wagon Train*, and, after such big budget cinematic hits as *McLintock!* (1963), he returned to television before helming *The Wild Geese*. The hot and dusty environs, large cast and action sequences must have felt like home territory for him.

An echo of James Bond runs through the film (in terms of personnel as opposed to tone). Moore provides an example of this right from the outset. In a violent scene, far removed from the jokey irreverence he brought to Ian Fleming's super-spy, he forces a young thug to eat a bag of 'bad' heroin, angered at being an unwitting courier of a drugs package which caused the death of a nineteen-year-old girl. No raised eyebrow here, though the film is littered with humour to offset the grimness of the mission itself. Production designer Syd Cain worked on previous Bond films including Moore's 1973 debut *Live and Let Die*. Editor and second unit director John Glen worked in the same post for Bond, having handled the famous ski-jump for the pre-credit sequence of *The Spy Who Loved Me* (1977). He would go on to helm all five of the official Eon Bond films in the '80s. Bob Simmons handles the action here as he did for past and future Bond films, as well as being the original silhouetted figure in the iconic Bond gun-barrel sequence. And Maurice Binder, whose title sequences became an iconic part of the 007 series, does a nice job with the titles here, setting the scene with images of soldiers fighting against the outline of a map of Africa before segueing into a child against the orange glow of the sun.

Heroic, romantic Gainsborough star Granger plays the merchant banker Sir Edward, and gives a high-powered turn as a man with corrupt influence everywhere. Burton's Faulkner takes no shit from him when he receives the offer of the contract, though we get the impression that he may not live if he turns it down. The sharpness of Burton is offset in the scene in which he is reunited with Harris' Janders after ten years. Despite their previous friendship, the former has no idea that Janders has a son named Emile, while the latter doesn't know Faulkner has been a widower for three years. Their reunion is awkward, with empathy coming from each in stuttering drips. Faulkner refers to Janders' "sparkling personality", and certainly the pair fire off each other with equal dominance of the screen.

The recruitment scenes are full of witty character business, such as Kenneth Griffiths' medic Arthur Witty (how apt!) asking if he has time to get a divorce. Given thirty-six hours, he replies: "Lovely, sir, I can't wait to see *his* face!" Compassion is also felt when Janders must tell

his son that their Swiss skiing holiday is off, the mission having been brought forward by three weeks. It's a tender moment, Rose scripting the characters as something more than mere cyphers.

This general complexity of character is further explored as Kruger's Coetzee expresses distaste at having to kill two hundred soldiers in the barracks that hold Limbani. He doesn't really like the black population of his country, but he doesn't particularly enjoy killing them. However, he denies himself the luxury of backing out of the mission because he needs the money to buy himself a quiet life, the consequences of his actions being something he'll learn to live with later. "I wonder how we'll stack up against each other morally?" he poses to Faulkner. Indeed, motivation for the mission seems to include anything from personal empire-rebuilding to the need at middle age to feel relevant. Saving the deposed president and helping him to realise his good intentions seems to play second fiddle for many of the mercenaries. How much are any of us prepared to pay for our own ambitions and causes?

The operation itself is a success, with the sentries taken out by Coetzee's cyanide-laced crossbows and Limbani freed. The editing here is particularly tight, with overhead and close-up shots lasting no more than seconds. However, back in London, Matherson has done a deal with General Ndofa, double-crossing the Wild Geese and saving himself £500,000 into the bargain, and all for a huge financial deal involving copper.

As the mercenaries attempt to flee the barracks and deliver Limbani to his own people with hopes of starting a civil war, their trucks are attacked on a bridge by Ndofa's

soldiers - the 'Simbas' - in a fighter plane. In one rather gruelling scene, Faulkner volunteers himself to shoot three badly wounded men rather than let them be taken by the Simbas.

As the surviving mercenaries splinter into two groups, Coetzee finds himself giving a piggy-back to Limbani owing to his weak heart. He frequently refers to the president as a kaffir, a South African racial slur derived from the Arabic word "non-believer". They eventually rest and exchange their opposing ideologies, with Coetzee declaring the white South Africans are there to stay. "I'm glad to hear that," Limbani replies, "then you'd better join us and help sort out our future… we have to forgive you for the past, and you have to forgive us for the present." Amid the chaos, it is a potent moment that finally addresses just what it really is all about, and Kruger and Ntshona (a South African playwright and Tony-winning actor) shine superbly.

_The Wild Geese_ was a particularly tough shoot for Burton. At the time of production, he was suffering from arthritis, gout and sciatica, and the medication taken for these ailments possibly caused more long-term damage. He was still drinking, though reckoned he was on top of his battle at this period, only drinking wine and occasional spirits in between a well regimented diet. Like his character, Burton remained dry whilst working. The scene where he uses two hands to raise a whisky glass was not due to delirium tremens but a trapped nerve pinching on his spine.

For Lloyd, the problem was not Burton's drinking but his bad back. As such, Lloyd was unable to get insurance for the actor - any problems, the $10 million feature would be crippled. You would never guess any of these issues during the film as Burton is seen fighting, jumping onto a plane, handling firearms and crashing to the ground throughout.

Likewise, Harris was known as a drinking hellraiser, though a deal was made that should he drink during filming, he would lose half his fee. He did fall off the wagon during the shoot in a shack christened the Red Ox, with Lloyd alerted to the Welsh singing, and promised it wouldn't happen again. Burton was livid and considered the act a massive insult.

Location filming took place in the Messina Border Region and Tshipise, Northern Transvaal (now Limpop), with interiors shot at the relatively small-scale Twickenham Studios by Richmond Film Productions (West). This Anglo-Swiss production company involved co-producers Erwin C. Dietrich, a Swiss film director, producer and actor; Douglas Netter, an American TV executive; and Chris Chrisafis, an American for whom this was his first production. Essentially, though, this was Lloyd's production.

I think what makes _The Wild Geese_ compelling is its richly drawn characters, who all seem very real and very flawed as a result. Coupled with this, its depth lies in the fact that the fictional narrative, though based loosely in truth, depicts a fight for a real and just cause no matter where individual motivations may reside. It also happens to a bloody well-made action film that delivers first class performances across the board. Its founding may have come from elsewhere before the source novel, and spawned lesser imitators, but _The Wild Geese_ stands on its own rather finely.

Euan Lloyd eventually produced a sequel, _Wild Geese II_, but that's another decade. In the meantime, dad, I hope you've enjoyed reading this as much as I enjoyed watching it thanks to your influence. Cheers!

# Beyond the Call of Friendship
# Miloš Forman's Hair

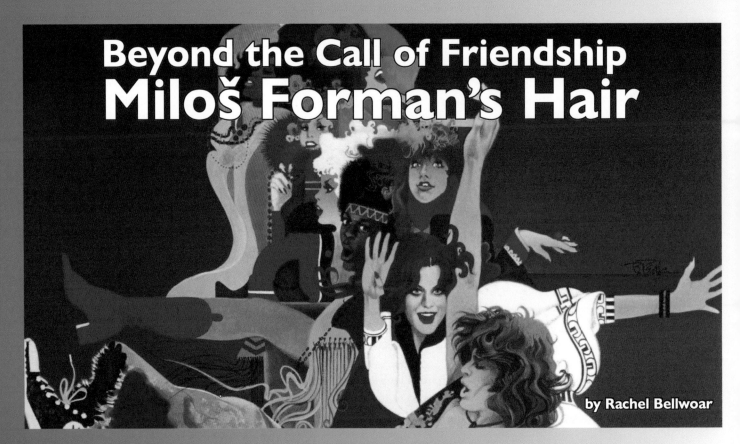

by Rachel Bellwoar

Getting drafted during the Vietnam War wasn't supposed to be a choice. In Miloš Forman's '70s film adaptation of the groundbreaking '60s musical *Hair*, Berger (Treat Williams) and his friends get sentenced to 30 days in a workhouse when they can't pay a $50 fine for crashing a party. That they wouldn't have enough "bread" to pay the $10,000 fine they could accrue for destroying their draft cards goes without saying, yet Berger doesn't seem the least bit worried.

Before he appears on-camera, Berger's voice can be heard reading the warning off his draft card about jail time. As Hud (Dorsey Wright), Jeannie (Annie Golden) and Woof (Donnie Dacus) set Berger's card on fire, his eyebrows wiggle and generally show what little concern he has for the possible blowback. They're in a tunnel at the time, and not only does the fire provide warmth, it is also essentially a light at the end of the tunnel. Breaking the law, rather than being a crime, becomes hope (albeit hope which can still end in destruction when the flames follow the tribe outside).

By comparison, Claude (John Savage) couldn't be more different. In the original musical created by Gerome Ragni and James Rado (who wrote the book and lyrics, with music by Galt MacDermot), Claude starts out a hippy too. But Michael Weller's screenplay places him as a newcomer in New York City, new to the peace-and-love lifestyle that Berger and his pals extol. In the opening moments, Claude can be seen boarding a bus to New York from Oklahoma, and his first reaction upon seeing the beatniks in Central Park is to stare. It's Berger who approaches him, asking

for cash, which Claude reluctantly tosses to him.

While Claude can be seen smiling and Berger doesn't seem to take the toss as an insult, this encounter differs from others Berger will have in the film with outsiders. For one thing, Berger usually never backs down. Whether that means inviting himself to a party attended by rich people, blocking the road to prevent a car passing by, or finding a way around security at a military base, he consistently stands his ground. That's why it's surprising he's prepared to walk away before Claude calls him back.

To be fair, while Claude's attire may mark him out as a tourist and much more buttoned-up than the colorful hippies (it's not at all surprising to learn that he plans to spend his time in New York visiting the Empire State Building and the Statue of Liberty), he's not especially rich or powerful, which could be why Berger doesn't press matters. Viewed in conjunction with how Berger treats Claude throughout the movie overall, it shows just how quickly Berger develops a soft spot for him - a soft spot that makes him vulnerable and more willing to forgive.

If everyone had a friend like George Berger, the world would be a better place, but why Claude is the beneficiary of this loyalty (and whether he deserves it) is a question which permeates throughout the movie version of *Hair*. Watching it for the first time, it's easy to get swept up in their bond and how quickly it forms. Claude is only staying in New York for a few days. He's meant to be joining the army and, unlike Berger, the idea that the draft should be a choice would never occur to him.

While Claude ultimately takes drugs and spends most of

his last few days with the tribe, the arrangement is always temporary. Try as Berger might to convince Claude that going in front of the draft board is folly, there's never really any doubt that Claude will answer the call to serve, even if it means getting killed. If anything, the impending deadline is why he pays Berger any attention. With the specter of death looming over him, Claude seizes the day. But would he have done so under normal circumstances? That's less clear.

There is a discrepancy, certainly, in how much Berger and the rest of the tribe are willing to do for Claude and what Claude is willing to do for them. This is proven by Claude's infatuation with Sheila (Beverly D'Angelo), a conventional love interest who comes from privilege and isn't initially part of the tribe either. Whether out of a desire to rebel against her parents or because she's charmed by Berger's dancing (it's her party the tribe crashes), Sheila's increasing interest in them means sticking with them, and this gives Claude a real shot at getting to know her.

Indeed, if it weren't for Berger acting as a wingman - which Claude never appreciates because he's too busy imagining him as a romantic rival - it's unlikely Shelia would've looked twice at him, yet for every good, selfless deed the tribe does, it's always the thought of Sheila that Claude puts foremost. He even thinks of Sheila when Jeannie proposes marriage to keep Claude out of the army (she's pregnant, and if he weds her with a baby on the way, he could avoid the draft).

It should be acknowledged that Claude is high when she proposes, so his lack of a reaction could be tied to that. But instead of turning her down, he says nothing which is about the cruelest thing he could do. Clearly he *is* listening, because what he hallucinates about his wedding day he imagines Sheila rather than Jeannie as his bride.

If acid trips are meant to be read the same way dreams are, then Claude's is very indicative of what his ideal future would be. Tellingly, the tribe aren't part of it. While Berger does show up in the hallucination, it's as a threat not a friend, trying to sidle up to Sheila and put the moves on her. Evidently, Sheila's attraction to Berger hasn't been lost on Claude, yet awareness isn't the same as acceptance. When Sheila reacts by flapping her hands to fly away, Forman cuts to Claude smiling.

To add insult to injury, Claude even imagines Sheila pregnant, but where Jeannie's pregnancy is surrounded by controversy (she doesn't even know who the father is), he envisages Sheila like a Virgin Mary who has been made pregnant with a kiss. In the end, Claude doesn't intend to let New York change him. He still craves a traditional marriage and the only person he wants to stay in contact with after leaving (and he does plan on leaving - that's proven when the wedding takes place at a church in Oklahoma) is Sheila, even though she's a stranger.

Change isn't always avoidable, though, and it's not until

the end that the unjustness of Claude's suspicions really hit home. It's also with the ending that *Hair* truly sets itself apart from the Broadway musical (and this is where, if you haven't seen the movie, it might be wise to stop reading).

It's easy to point to the song *Manchester England* as the moment *Hair* starts the laying the groundwork for Berger's sacrifice. It's the song, after all, that Berger reprises in his final scene. The first time it's heard is when Claude is high, and Berger starts to sing about him. "Claude Hooper Bukowski finds that it's groovy to hide in a movie," Berger sings, before comparing Claude to directors like Fellini and Antonioni. Claude is far from the director in this scene - it's Berger who is, at one point picking Claude up like a puppet, to be spun around and controlled.

Eventually Claude takes over, so instead of Berger singing "That's him" the lyrics change to "That's me." Ultimately, Berger's insistence on interfering in Claude's life will bring about his downfall. Not many people would drive cross country from New York to Nevada to see a friend off. What makes Berger and the tribe's gesture all the more moving (if boggling) is that 'friend' is such a generous term to describe Claude.

Yet perhaps that's the one thing Berger and Claude

have in common. Usually showing concern for strangers is painted in a positive or philanthropic light, yet in Hud's fiancée's song, *Easy to be Hard* (and unfortunately, she's never given her own name) she specifically calls out: "Especially people who care about strangers... Do you only care about the bleeding crowd? How about a needing friend?"

Claude and Berger are devoted to strangers. In Claude's case, while Sheila only decided to tag along at the last minute, she's the first person Claude asks about when Berger shows up at the military base. She's the only person he really spends any time with when Berger agrees to pose as him so he can make the time say goodbye. What Berger does for Claude in turn, however, goes beyond the call of friendship (and beyond what Berger initially meant to give).

Watching the ending of *Hair* never gets easier. Even when you know what's coming, it's just too painful. Part of that has to do with Forman and Weller not employing any tricks. Claude doesn't get a flat tire. He doesn't lose track of time. He returns at a reasonable hour, but it doesn't matter. For whatever reason, the army chose that day to deploy and it's Berger who is sent to Vietnam instead of Claude.

This swap doesn't happen in the Broadway show, but it's one of cinema's greatest gut-punch endings. Watching Treat Williams as Berger try to figure out what to do is unbearable, as it happens so fast. Berger can't change his mind. Once he doesn't speak-up, it's over.

*Hair* opens with Berger and the tribe exiting a tunnel. It ends with Berger entering the dark void of the aircraft as Claude Bukowski. Berger gets his name back (it appears on his gravestone during *The Flesh Failures/Let the Sunshine In*), but he loses everything else.

# MANNAJA

by Joe Secrett

By the late '70s, the spaghetti western genre was fading away. Few productions were being made, the sets were crumbling, and the directors and actors were moving into new trends. Since the early '70s, gialli and Eurocrime films had been growingly successful, and the result was that westerns had been pushed into the shadows.

Spaghetti westerns had undergone a strange, drastic change a few years earlier which had prolonged the life of the genre. This was the emergence of a comedy-western hybrid, popular for a time thanks to the success of the Bud Spencer/Terence Hill *Trinity* films. These light-hearted entries replaced fast and vicious gunfights with slapstick fisticuffs. At the same time, the kung fu genre was taking off around the world and many actors from kung fu movies found themselves playing heroes or villains in spaghetti westerns. The entertaining *The Fighting Fists of Shanghai Joe* (1973), for example, had Chen Lee co-starring with Klaus Kinski, while *The Stranger and the Gunfighter* (1974) cast Lo Lieh alongside Lee Van Cleef (Lieh was the star of *King Boxer*, aka *Five Fingers of Death* [1972], one of the biggest kung fu films of the early '70s and a key title in the explosion of the martial arts genre in the United States).

By the late '70s, spaghettis were in decline in all forms. It didn't matter whether they were comical or serious, action-packed or psychological. The genre was dwindling fast. Some adapted as best as they could to the changing landscape, tossing more nudity and violence into the mix and, in some cases, scaling back the comedic elements. There were even occasional novel curiosities like the softcore sex entry *Porno-Erotic Western* (1979).

Aptly nicknamed 'twilight spaghettis', these final offerings were often brutal and nihilistic in tone, and were populated by dubious characters who were rarely, if ever, motivated by good intentions. Like their '60s counterparts, the twilight spaghettis followed a defined formula, but now the formula had shifted considerably since the early days. The emphasis on violence, cruelty and destruction was greater than ever. Other genres had ramped-up graphic content (blood-spurting bullet wounds, limbs being lopped off, etc.), and the makers of these westerns had no intention of being outdone in the bloodshed department.

All of which brings me to an Italian entry which is one of the best-known twilight westerns. In fact, *Mannaja*, aka *A Man Called Blade* (1977), might be the darkest of the lot.

Many suspicious characters are involved in this tale of a man looking for vengeance and profit. The opening shows our hero (or anti-hero, depending how you look at it) capturing his bounty, Burt Craven (Donal O'Brien). This opening sequence takes place in a muddy, misty swamp, and contains the sort of increased violence that we'll see plenty of throughout the feature - in this case, Craven's gun hand is chopped off with a well-timed hatchet throw.

Blade (Maurizio Merli) attempts to get his reward for Craven from a mining town called Suttonville, a dark, dank, muddy place reminiscent of the town in Sergio Corbucci's *Django*. When he learns the town has no sheriff and there's no chance of him claiming the reward money, he accepts a job from the local mine owner McGowan (Phillipe Leroy), who wants someone to track down his daughter who was taken by bandits. After earning the ire of McGowan's right-hand man Voller (John Steiner) at a card game, Blade is dragged into a scheme about a possible takeover of the mine by outside forces.

Eurocrime stalwart Merli had been enjoying considerable success due to his likeness to international superstar Franco Nero. Merli amassed a sizeable number of roles, especially in police action dramas like *The Iron Commissioner* (1978) where he played a tough, two-fisted cop who bends the rules to get his man. While his character's name might have been different from one cop film to the next, their personality remained essentially the same. The films were hugely profitable, coming at a time when crime rates and corruption were rampant, and cinema-goers got a thrill out of seeing screen criminals getting their just desserts.

*Mannaja* contains an undercurrent of dread throughout, emphasised by the locale and characters. The town is rarely seen without fog, apart from one raging gun battle sequence (after which it returns to its gloomy, almost post-apocalyptic look). The set itself was falling apart at the time, so the use of fog was possibly necessary to disguise its dilapidated state. Also, there is mud everywhere - there's barely an inch of dry ground in this town and everyone is always dirty and filthy. McGowan has had his men working in poor conditions at the mine, and they too look straggly and filthy.

The soundtrack by Guido and Maurizio De Angelis fits the grim tone very well. The main theme, *Wolf*, is a sombre tune with incredibly deep vocals which pretty much describe Blade's life and actions. There are biblical undertones in some tracks - one song, aptly named *Snake*, details the betrayal of a major character, and the lyrics seem to anticipate the fate of said character: "Something's gonna happen very soon, just wait and see." The entire soundtrack combines horror-type synths with an almost folksy style of acoustic accompaniment.

The editing throughout is adept, but several scenes particularly stand out. One example is when some female dancers arrive to entertain the town. At the same time, a stagecoach is robbed and its occupants murdered. We see the girls dancing away to upbeat, cheerful tones with quick intercut shots of each occupant of the stagecoach holdup being brutally slain, squibs and all. The sequence is deliberately jarring, reminding us that no-one is safe, that no-one can be certain of surviving to the film's end.

The wealth of Euro stars in *Mannaja* elevate it above other westerns of this type, none more so than Phillipe Leroy as the wheelchair-bound McGowan. He's great as a religious puritan who finds himself at odds with Blade and his own right-hand man Voller, The latter is impeccably

played by British actor John Steiner (who sadly died in 2022 in a car accident). He makes a great villainous foil, portraying Voller as a German-accented, well-dressed thug, always accompanied by two attack dogs and a group of gunmen loyal to him and McGowan. The outlaw Burt Craven, captured by Blade in the opening scene, is played by another genre stalwart, Donal O'Brien, who had appeared in the popular *Run, Man, Run* (1968). He has one of those familiar faces which viewers recognise without necessarily knowing him by name. He loses his shooting hand in this opening sequence, but returns with ulterior motives during the last half of the feature, keeping us guessing whose side he's actually on.

*Mannaja* is helmed by Sergio Martino, whose previous western was the lesser-known *Arizona Colt Returns* (1970) starring Anthony Steffen. Martino had also directed one of the pivotal Eurocrime films of the decade, *The Violent Professionals* (1973), and the seminal giallo *Torso* (1973). He skillfully keeps us guessing who will come out on top of the various encounters. Even though Blade is skilled, he endures more trials and tribulations than a standard, run-of-the-mill action hero, being beaten, blown up, tortured and, in a notorious scene supposedly cut from some releases, buried up to his neck with spikes holding his eyes open as he faces the baking sun.

*Mannja* has been accused of being a clone of another Italian western from the previous year, Enzo G Castellari's *Keoma* (1976). It's true that both films share similar aspects - the foggy, apocalyptic-looking locale; a soundtrack by Guido and Maurizio De Angelis which has the same style of vocals (by the same singer, no less); the gothic, gloomy

cinematography. Both share the same bleak, downtrodden atmosphere, and it's not much of a stretch to imagine them existing in the same cinematic universe.

One thing is certain - *Mannaja* is an interesting Italian western, very different from the American counterparts being released at that time. With skillful direction from Martino, and enough twists to fill a whodunit book, it's a prime example from the genre's twilight years.

# STAR CRASH

Determined to crash the sci-fi boom at the movies, Italy turned to giallo maestro Luigi Cozzi to create a cash cow with a goofy entry called *Starcrash*.

Kevin Nickelson explores further…

"A long time ago in a galaxy far, far away…"

Those ten simple words were used on the opening scrawl for George Lucas' industry-altering *Star Wars*. Ten words which lit a fuse and caused a cascading explosion across the world box office in 1977. Not only did *Star Wars* set cash registers afire everywhere, not only did it spark the imagination of starry-eyed fans across the spectrum, it also inspired cinema industries around the world to scramble to find knock-offs of their own to ride the coat-tails of its stellar success The Italians especially were always on the lookout for a bandwagon to board. They were among the first to step forward with one of the wildest pulp adventures to ever wield a laser.

American father-son producers Nat and Patrick Waschberger, of Film Enterprises Productions, approached the Italian director Luigi Cozzi at the Cannes Film Festival in May 1977 to suggest doing a variation on *Star Wars*. Cozzi shot a small amount of test footage and showed it to the pair, convincing them he was the right man for the job.

I interviewed Cozzi at the 2018 Festival of Fantastic Films in Manchester, England, where he elaborated: "The genesis was *Star Wars*. At the movies, at that time, *Star Wars* was big. I hadn't seen the picture because it hadn't opened in Europe yet - there was a six-month delay. But they had published the script as a novelization about two years before, and I'd bought a copy with the Ralph McQuarrie cover. That cover by McQuarrie - I wanted it; it was so beautiful! So, I bought it and added it to my collection. One day, the producer called me and said he wanted a *Star Wars* imitation. At this point, I still hadn't seen the movie… but I thought, what the hell, I have the novelization! So, I grabbed the book and I read it. It was very easy - two hours to read in full. I realized where Lucas had taken his sources. Many were from Robert Heinlein's juvenile books, which had sold a million copies in the early '50s in America. The last of them was 'Starship Troopers'. The first ones had a young hero who was like Luke Skywalker. He does some fantastic enterprise, then discovers he is not the son of a couple he believes are his parents, but rather the son of the richest family in the world. I decided to do something inspired by the Heinlein books, directly. I avoided *Star Wars*. I wanted to do it differently. I noticed both Heinlein and Lucas had a young boy as hero but I wanted a girl, because in most of my pictures the hero is the girl. *La Portiera Nuda* is a girl. *The Killer Must Kill Again* has a young girl. *Alien Contamination* is a lady."

The plot deals with an overlord Emperor (Christopher Plummer) who recruits renegade smuggler Stella Star

(Caroline Munro) and her associates for a mission to rescue the leader's son from the clutches of a powerful, evil count and his army. What ensues is an amalgam of derring-do action, optical effects and stop-motion animation which wows the audience. Given a budget just above $4 million by FEP, Cozzi carried out principal photography at the Cinecitta Studios in Rome before capturing the rest on location in Morocco, Tunisia and California. He chose to utilise some dazzling stop-motion wizardry that some filmmakers might have shied away from. Cozzi saw it as a chance to pay tribute to the legendary special effects guru Ray Harryhausen. In an interview with the Dutch fanzine 'Schokkend Nieuws', he spoke of Harryhausen and his indirect influence on the movie: "I never got to meet him, but I did exchange letters with him at the time of making *Starcrash*. I love stop-motion and I wanted to tell him that we were doing stop-motion scenes in our movie. He wrote back, saying he would love to see the film. It was very difficult to do the stop-motion in *Starcrash*, because nobody in Italy was doing it. I had to find people who knew how it was done, people who had the same machinery that Harryhausen had. We used an East German machine, a stop-motion projector, alongside a stop-motion camera. These enabled me to do the Harryhausen-style effects alone and cheaply. But the trouble was nobody was using it, except Karel Zeman in Czechoslovakia, who was making beautiful pictures, and Harryhausen himself. I knew it was no use asking Harryhausen to come and work on *Starcrash*, because he didn't even want to go work for George Lucas when he asked. We tried to hire

91

Dave Allen from the United States, but it turned out to be too complicated. He needed to move all his equipment. In the end, we found a guy in France. He was not as good as Dave Allen, but it was easier to hire him."

It was through Harryhausen, however, that Cozzi was able to hire Munro to play the heroine Stella Star. The director was happy, and surprised, to land her. "She was gorgeous. I thought it was impossible. I told the producer she would be perfect for it, but I never thought we could get her. Then suddenly he told me he'd got that girl I wanted. Turned out it was easy! Caroline was terrific. A perfect professional. Very British. Between shots, she was knitting! On the screen she is really tough, but in real life she is quiet, a very nice lady. And she was excited to be in the film."

Early in the process, American International Pictures purchased distribution rights. Due to the immense success at the box office of their 1976 feature *The Food of the Gods*, the company insisted on a leading role for its new breakout star Marjoe Gortner. This ended up creating significant problems for Cozzi, who explained: "He [Marjoe] was a friend of Sam Arkoff's son. They said: 'Marjoe will play Akton.' Actually, in my script the character was an alien. What I had in mind was like the mutant from *This Island Earth*. But Marjoe didn't like it. He wanted no makeup on his face. I tried and tried, but the producer said: 'No makeup!' Then I decided to change his character, to give him powers. Otherwise, he would just be a meaningless character. I mean, why would Stella Star even need him? She could get along fine without him. So, I made him into a sort of Peter Pan."

The filming process must have been memorable if an icon of Christopher Plummer's stature could recall it many years later. He did so, rather fondly (in a bit of a left-handed way), for an interview on October 7th, 2013 carried out by Will Harris of avclub.com. "There are two things I can say about that film [*Starcrash*]," Plummer remarked. "One, give me Rome any day. I'd do a porno in Rome if it meant I could get to Rome! I think I spent about three days there on *Starcrash*. It was all shot at once. And the girl, Caroline Munro… she was something incredible to look at! That was a great pleasure, too. Beyond those two things, how do you play the Emperor of the Universe? I mean, it's a wonderful part to play! It puts God in a very dicey moment, doesn't it? He's very insecure, God, when the Emperor's around!"

The picture also featured the first motion picture role for a then-little-known actor named David Hasselhoff, who plays the Emperor's son, Prince Simon. Years prior to driving Kitt the high-tech talking car in *Knight Rider* or mingling with the bikini beauties of *Baywatch*, Hasselhoff found himself tussling with aliens and engaging in spaceship battles in this Italian space opera. Did Cozzi sense his star potential at the time? "I was sent videocassettes with many young actors from soap operas," he commented. "When I saw David, for me, he was perfect. I wanted that face, that beauty! I didn't see if he may be a good actor, or could become a star."

The icing on the cake is the flavorful score by master composer John Barry, who would go on to win an award at France's Festival du Cinema Fantastique for his music. Better still, *Starcrash* was nominated for Best International Film at the seventh annual Saturn Film Awards. According to the American Film Institute, it amassed $475,000 in its first week of release and more than $2.25 million in U.S. domestic rentals for the year.

*Starcrash* endures in popularity because audiences continue to get that it is meant to be tongue-in-cheek, that they are being kidded. Heck, the film kids itself! The inclusion of humorous moments was entirely intentional from the start. Cozzi told me: "Of course it's a joke! If you imagine a suspense scene with a bomb, all the way back to Hitchcock with the bomb on the bus [in *Sabotage*], there are numerous ways such a scene can play out. They can find the bomb. They can throw it away. They can diffuse it. It could explode. But in *Starcrash*, the Emperor turns up and says: 'I am the Emperor of the Galaxy! What is *time* to me? I can stop it!' I've seen dozens of scenes in other movies with bombs, and my solution to that problem is absurd. *Starcrash* is filled with absurdities, because that is what I liked about the movies I watched from the '50. I think I went beyond it."

Fun and absurd, and intentionally so, *Starcrash* remains a cult favorite to this day.

**"It's gonna take you and the police department and the fire department and the National Guard to get me outta here" - Sally Field embraces the union and fights for her rights in**

# Norma Rae

### by Jonathon Dabell

Director Martin Ritt was particularly good at making films about people caught up in challenging and tumultuous times and events. *Edge of the City* (1957) tackled difficult interracial friendships among New York dockworkers; *Five Branded Women* (1960) followed five disgraced females cast out from their town in Yugoslavia during WWII who try to redeem themselves by fighting alongside the partisans; *Hud* (1963) examined the conflict between a Texan patriarch and his son during a catastrophic outbreak of foot-and-mouth disease which threatens the existence of their ranch; *The Molly Maguires* (1970) looked at masculine loyalty and appalling working conditions in a Pennsylvanian coal mine in the 19th century. He worked in other genres too, often successfully, but for my money he was always at his best making dramas which tackled big social, historical or political dilemmas.

Ritt first became interested in making *Norma Rae* in the mid '70s after reading an article by Henry P. Leifermann about a female cotton mill worker who had tried to unionise the workers at the J.P. Stevens textile factory where she worked. Named Crystal Lee Sutton, she had been inspired by a labour organiser named Eli Zivkovich to demand better pay for the work she was doing and safer conditions in which to carry out her duties. She was ultimately fired from her job, but did a great deal to raise the profile of the Textile Workers Union of America. Thanks to her activism, many of her fellow workers came to understand they had a right to expect better standards and benefits from their bosses.

Leifermann eventually expanded his article into a book, called 'Crystal Lee: A

Woman of Inheritance'. Both the original article and the book provided Ritt with the nucleus for his movie. He appointed the man-and-wife team Irving Ravetch and Harriet Frank Jr. (who had scripted several of his earlier movies) to write a screenplay based on Crystal Lee's story. As the story took shape, it became less like a biopic and more like a fictional story with passing similarities to what had happened at Crystal Lee's textiles plant. The real Crystal Lee Sutton was somewhat misadvised about what payment she could expect if a movie was made about her story. Only many years later did she belatedly receive a financial settlement to acknowledge the fact her actions had provided the basis for the film.

The screen version introduces a character very like Crystal Lee, here named Norma Rae Wilson. She is played by Sally Field, who, despite being at a fairly early point in her career, delivers a knockout performance which scooped virtually every major award going that year, including a Best Actress at Cannes, a Golden Globe and an Academy Award. Norma Rae works in the textiles mill in her local town in the Deep South, alongside her mother Leona (Barbara Baxley), father Vernon (Pat Hingle) and most of her friends. It's the kind of town where almost every family has at least one member employed at the mill. In many cases, the whole family work there, and generation after generation follow their parents into the same line of employment at the same site without a second thought.

As the movie opens, Norma Rae is worried to find her mother suffering from spells of deafness, probably caused by the incredibly noisy working environment. This being a time before bosses and executives had to worry about health and safety regulations, Norma Rae is told to quit her squawking and get back to work. It's the same for everyone - the effect of the environment, the workload, the length of the working day, the unsafe conditions, etc. are ignored by those at the top. All that matters is that every worker is pushed to their limit day in, day out, for the measliest of salaries.

Enter a Jewish union represent from New York, Reuben Warshowsky (Ron Leibman), who has been sent to this backwater corner of the South to raise awareness of the Textile Workers Union of America and what it could do to improve pay and conditions. Warshowsky is dismayed to find most of the workers indifferent towards him. They seem to have an inherent distrust of Jews, outsiders and unions - and he embodies all three. He gets the overriding sense that those who work in the mill are too afraid to rock the boat by demanding better standards. They fear authority and need the money their job provides. As far as they are concerned, unions exist purely to cause trouble and don't make any progress in terms of bringing about positive changes. They're certainly not willing to risk their livelihood by joining his union.

Knowing he faces an uphill struggle, maybe even an

impossible task, Warshowsky singles out Norma Rae as someone who might be useful to have on his side. He slowly and patiently helps her recognise everything that is wrong about her place of work, and gently guides her into becoming his union spokesperson inside the plant. It helps that Norma Rae is already unhappy about her mother's deteriorating hearing, and when her father dies of a heart attack in the factory after having his complaints of chest pain cursorily dismissed, she grows even more determined to campaign for change.

On top of all this, Norma Rae is a mother to two illegitimate kids, and becomes the stepmom to a further child when she marries single father Sonny (Beau Bridges), a good, loyal man who stands by her for who she is. As she becomes a growing thorn in the side of her employers, they try to besmirch Norma Rae's name by dragging up her past promiscuity and other ugly truths that paint her in an unflattering light.

Eventually, Norma Rae's mouth gets too big for the liking of her bosses and they fire her. But, in one of the most iconic scenes in '70s cinema (based on an incident that happened with the real Crystal Lee Sutton), she refuses to leave the factory. Instead, she stands on a workstation holding a hand-scrawled sign displaying the word 'UNION' and makes it clear to everyone she is going nowhere. Every one of her fellow millworkers contemplates whether to shut off their machine to show solidarity for what Norma

Rae stands for. Slowly, painstakingly, they decide to cut their machines. The mill falls silent. Every man and woman in the building flips the lever to show their support for Norma Rae. She may have lost her job, but she has won the fight. The bosses have no choice but to put the right to unionise to a vote. The result is tight, but the workers opt to sign up with the union.

Norma Rae works because of the excellent writing by Ravetch and Frank Jr., the unobtrusive direction by Ritt, and the quality of the performances. Field is the obvious standout because she's the focal point of the story, the character in whose struggle we become invested. It would be a mistake to underestimate the contribution of the others, especially Leibman as the dedicated union man fighting an uphill struggle in a town where he is initially unwanted and ignored, and Bridges as the oft-neglected husband who makes enormous sacrifices so his wife can pursue her beliefs.

The factory environment is brilliantly captured. Ritt chose to shoot interiors at a real mill in Opelika, Alabama. The mill had been unionised, and the director admitted it would have been impossible to take his cameras into a factory where unionisation had not yet been embraced, as there would have been considerable opposition from the bosses and much of the workforce. The noise of the machines, the heat and sweat of the working day, the monotony of the job, the gulf between the top brass and the lowly workers - it's all splendidly captured by Ritt and the legendary cinematographer John A. Alonzo.

Critics at the time were largely impressed and audience reaction was favourable. Norma Rae was a modest hit in 1979, initially making $22 million against its $4.5 million budget. Columbia, Warner Brothers and United Artists must all have kicked themselves for turning Ritt down when he came to them seeking financing for the film. 20th Century Fox only agreed to back it when the director assured them it would be an uplifting and motivational story, not some drab and dreary wallow in miserable working class lives. Ritt had the last laugh though, with Norma Rae receiving a Best Picture Oscar nomination and proving itself an enduring tale about guts, determination and inspiration. There was also an Oscar win for the song It Goes Like It Goes, composed by David Shire, sung by Jennifer Warnes with lyrics by Norman Gimbel. The film was placed on a list created by the 'New York Times' in 2003 to name the Best 1000 Movies Ever.

As working-class heroes and heroines go, Norma Rae (the character) is right up there with the best of 'em. And Norma Rae (the movie) is one of the essential titles of its type.

# CLOSING CREDITS

### Simon J. Ballard
Simon lives in Oxford and works in its oldest building, a Saxon Tower. Whilst also working in the adjoining church, he has never felt tempted to re-enact scenes from *Taste the Blood of Dracula* or *Dracula A.D.1972*. He has never done this. Ever. He regularly contributes to the magazine 'We Belong Dead' and its various publications, and once read Edgar Allan Poe's 'The Black Cat' to a garden full of drunk young people at his local gay pub The Jolly Farmers. His first published work was a Top Tip in 'Viz' of which he is justifiably proud.

### Rachel Bellwoar
Rachel is a writer for 'Comicon', 'Diabolique' magazine and 'Flickering Myth'. If she could have any director fim a biopic about her life it would be Aki Kaurismäki.

### Dawn Dabell
Dawn runs her own clothing business in West Yorkshire. When she's not busy selling fabulous dresses and quirky tops, she's a full-time film enthusiast, writer and mum! She has written for 'Cinema Retro', 'We Belong Dead', 'Monster!' and 'Weng's Chop', and is also the co-author of 'More Than a Psycho: The Complete Films of Anthony Perkins' (2018) and 'Ultimate Warrior: The Complete Films of Yul Brynner' (2019). She is also the co-creator and designer of the very mag you're holding in your hands right now.

### Jonathon Dabell
Jonathon was born in Nottingham in 1976. He is a huge film fan and considers '70s cinema his favourite decade. He has written for 'Cinema Retro' and 'We Belong Dead', and co-authored 'More Than a Psycho: The Complete Films of Anthony Perkins' and 'Ultimate Warrior: The Complete Films of Yul Brynner' with his wife. He lives in Yorkshire with his wife, three kids, three cats and two rabbits!

### David Flack
David was born and bred in Cambridge. He has had reviews published in 'We Belong Dead' and 'Cinema of the '80s'. He loves watching, talking, reading and writing about film and participating on film forums. The best film he has seen in over 55 years of watching is *Jaws* (1975). The worst is *The Creeping Terror* (1963) or anything by Andy Milligan.

### Brian Gregory
Brian is an English tutor who both reviews and makes films in his spare time. He has his first horror feature film currently in post-production. He has written several articles for 'We Belong Dead'. Originally from North Harrow, Brian now resides in Hove, Sussex. Among his favourite '70s films would be: *High Plains Drifter*, *Scum*, *Annie Hall*, *Phase IV* and *The Tenant*. His website is www.gregoryfilms.co.uk

### John Harrison
John is a Melbourne, Australia-based freelance writer and film historian who has written for numerous genre publications, including 'Fatal Visions', 'Cult Movies', 'Is It Uncut?', 'Monster!' and 'Weng's Chop'. Harrison is also the author of the Headpress book 'Hip Pocket Sleaze: The Lurid World of Vintage Adult Paperbacks', has recorded audio commentaries for Kino Lorber, and composed the booklet essays for the Australian Blu-ray releases of *Thirst*, *Dead Kids* and *The Survivor*. 'Wildcat!', Harrison's book on the film and television career of former child evangelist Marjoe Gortner, was published by Bear Manor in 2020.

### Kev Hurst
Kev is a Nottingham FE college teacher of film and animation and a historian of all things cinematic. He is a massive physical film and TV collector who spends way too much time browsing the shelves of his local CEX store. He is an avid fan of all genres but has passionate interests in all things horror and sci-fi related, from body horror to giallo, dystopian fiction to steampunk. His favourite filmmakers are basically all 'The Movie Brats' and well-respected horror directors like John Carpenter, David Cronenberg, John Landis, Dario Argento, Mario Bava, Tobe Hooper and George A. Romero.

### Bryan C. Kuriawa
Based in New Jersey, Bryan has spent many years diving into the world of movies. Introduced to the Three Stooges by his grandfather and Japanese cinema when he was eight, he's wandered on his own path, ignoring popular opinions. Willing to discuss and defend everything from Jesus Franco's surreal outings to the 007 masterpiece *Moonraker*, nothing is off-limits. Some of his favorite filmmakers include Ishiro Honda, Jacques Tati, Lewis Gilbert, Jesus Franco and Jun Fukuda.

### James Lecky
James is an actor, writer and occasional stand-up comedian who has had a lifelong obsession with cinema, beginning with his first visit to the Palace Cinema in Derry (now long since gone) to see *Chitty Chitty Bang Bang* when he was six. Since then, he has happily wallowed in cinema of all kinds but has a particular fondness for Hammer movies, spaghetti westerns, Euro-crime and samurai films.

### Darren Linder
Darren grew up in the '70s and has been forever enamored with films from that decade. He is a lifelong resident of Oregon, currently living in Portland. He has performed in many rock bands, ran a non-profit dog rescue, and worked in social service with at-risk youths. Currently he works security in music venues, and is completing a book about his experiences there to be published soon. His favorite film directors of the '70s are Sam Peckinpah, Francis Ford Coppola and William Friedkin.

### Stephen Mosley

Stephen is an actor and writer, whose books include 'Christopher Lee: The Loneliness of Evil' (Midnight Marquee Press), 'Klawseye: The Imagination Snatcher of Phantom Island', 'The Lives & Deaths of Morbius Mozella', 'TOWN' and 'The Boy Who Loved Simone Simon'. His film articles have appeared in such magazines as 'Midnight Marquee', 'We Belong Dead' and 'The Dark Side'. His film credits include the evil Ear Goblin in *Kenneth*; the eponymous paranormal investigator of *Kestrel Investigates*; the shady farmer, James, in *Contradiction*; and a blink-and-you'll-miss-it appearance opposite Sam Neill in *Peaky Blinders*. Stephen is one half of the music duo Collinson Twin and lives in a dungeon near Leeds.

### Kevin Nickelson

Kevin has been a fan of cinema of all genres and decades since age 4. As he grew older he found his passions for dissecting various aspects of film and decided to marry this obsession with his ability for creative writing into writing about film. Kevin has written for 'Scarlet the Magazine', the 'Van Helsing Confidential' and the site classic-horror.com. Currently, he writes for 'We Belong Dead' magazine and books, 'Scary Monsters' magazine, horrornews.net and will soon be working for 'Scream' magazine. Kevin is also co-host of the Grim and Bloody podcast produced by Death's Parade Film Fest.

### Peter Sawford

Peter was born in Essex in 1964 so considers himself a child of the '70s. A self-confessed film buff, he loves watching, reading about and talking about cinema. A frustrated writer his whole life, he's only recently started submitting what he writes to magazines. His favourite director is Alfred Hitchcock with Billy Wilder running him a close second. He still lives in Essex with his wife and works as an IT trainer and when not watching films he's normally panicking over who West Ham are playing next.

### Joseph Secrett

Joseph is a film nut and collector who started at a young age, and quickly became infatuated with all things cinematic. He is a huge fan of 20th century cinema, especially the '60s and '70s for their sheer diversity of genres. Top choices of his include revisionist westerns and seedy crime dramas.

### Aaron Stielstra

Aaron was born in Ann Arbor, Michigan and grew up in Tucson, AZ. and NYC. He is an actor, writer, illustrator, soundtrack composer and director. After moving to Italy in 2012, he has appeared in 4 spaghetti westerns and numerous horror-thrillers - all of them unnecessarily wet. He recently directed the punk rock comedy *Excretion: the Shocking True Story of the Football Moms*. His favorite '70s actor is Joe Spinell.

### Ian Taylor

Ian dabbled in horror fiction in the early '90s before writing and editing music fanzines. He later adjudicated plays for the Greater Manchester Drama Federation but enjoys film analysis most. Over the last five years, he has become a regular writer and editorial team member for 'We Belong Dead' magazine and contributed to all their book releases. This has led to writing for Dez Skinn's 'Halls of Horror', Allan Bryce's 'Dark Side' and Hemlock's 'Fantastic Fifties', amongst others. His first solo book 'All Sorts of Things Might Happen: The Films of Jenny Agutter' was recently released as a 'We Belong Dead' publication.

### Dr. Andrew C. Webber

Dr. W. has been a Film, Media and English teacher and examiner for over 35 years and his passion for the cinema remains undiminished all these years later. As far as he is concerned, a platform is where you wait for the 08.16 to Victoria; dropping is something that louts do with litter; and streaming is how you might feel if you were in *Night of the Hunter* being hotly pursued by Robert Mitchum with "Hate" tattooed on his knuckles and Stanley Cortez doing the cinematography.

### Steven West

Steven's first published work was as a floppy haired teenager, voice breaking as he scribbled about Terence Fisher for an early issue of 'We Belong Dead' - a useful break from the lingerie section of the Freeman's catalogue. He still writes for the magazine and its spin offs while regularly contributing to 'The Fantastic Fifties' magazine and the UK Frightfest website, alongside www.horrorscreamsvideovault.co.uk. In 2019, Auteur Publishing released his 'Devil's Advocate' book about Wes Craven's *Scream*. Steven lives in Norfolk with his partner, daughter and - thanks to permanent home working - a dozen sock-puppet 'friends'.

Printed in Great Britain
by Amazon

20422742R00058